Status Terminology and the Social Structure
of North American Indians

THE AMERICAN ETHNOLOGICAL SOCIETY

Verne F. Ray, Editor

Status Terminology and the Social Structure of North American Indians

By MUNRO S. EDMONSON

1958

UNIVERSITY OF WASHINGTON PRESS

Seattle

115958

Lithographed in the United States of America

Acknowledgments

THE WRITER is indebted to his colleagues on the staff of the Urban Life Research Institute of Tulane University for assistance in the solution of many problems incident to this study, and especially to Dr. Robert C. Stone, Dr. Cliff W. Wing, Jr. , and Dr. E. Lee Hoffman. Gratitude is also due to Dr. Forrest LaViolette of the Department of Sociology and Anthropology of Tulane University for helpful criticisms and suggestions.

ACKNOWLEDGEMENTS

Contents

1. Introduction

ANTHROPOLOGICAL descriptions of social structure face
certain problems of method which are not so sharply raised
for the student of our own Western European culture. Among
these problems is the necessity of beginning almost from
scratch with a description of a foreign social system in
which even the most obvious and commonplace of social statuses becomes strange and requires primary definition. In
attempting to deal with this problem anthropologists have
developed with little explicit theorizing a fairly standard
method for describing the phenomenon of status. Thus we
may find again and again in anthropological monographs
statements of the form: the Eskimo shaman or angakok has
such and such rights and duties; his patterns of behavior follow such and such ideals; failure to perform in the pre-
scribed manner results in such and such sanctions while
success brings certain named rewards; he typically occupies
certain other statuses (male, hunter, etc.); his actual behavior deviates from the ideal in particular respects, and so
on. The ad hoc nature of these anthropological descriptions
and the "natural" way in which they seem to fit the data have
long obscured the fundamental discovery to which they point,
namely, that any social system may be described in terms
of the statuses which make it up, the patterned expectations
adhering to those statuses, the norms of and for behavior
and the permissible alternatives and deviations from them,
the rewards and punishments which presumably motivate
such behavior, and the functional and historical structural
relationships between statuses. We have discovered, in
short, the phenomenon of status.

The process of explication of this discovery has taken a
long time. Without attempting to trace in detail the development of anthropological ideas of social organization, we may
mention Durkheim's (1947) formulation of social solidarity
as derivative of shared conceptions of rights and duties,
Linton's summary treatment of the concepts of status and
role (1936:113-31), Lowie's summary work on social organization (1920 and 1948), and Murdock's extensive comparative analysis (1949) as major contributions to this process.
In significant respects, however, the discovery of the uni-
versality of status as a fundamental unit in social structure
comes as a result of the descriptive ethnographic work of
anthropological field investigators in various parts of the
world over a period of more than fifty years.

The concept of status in modern social science is derived
from the legal field, but it has undergone important changes
in meaning in the derivation. The legal definition of the term
is more restricted, referring to the legal position of an individual not derived from contract--especially where such a
position is derivative of family relationships. Thus Maine's
Ancient Law (1873:XL) states: "The tie between man and
man which replaces those rights and duties which have their
origin in the family is contract. It was the tendency of former law to fix the condition of 'status' of persons by positive
rules; in modern times, the condition of persons is commonly the immediate or remote result of agreement. The movement has been from status to contract."

Maine was concerned with a quasi-evolutionary progres-
sion from status to contract law, a point which he makes
clear in attempting to give explicit definition to the concept
status: "The word Status may be usefully employed to con-
struct a formula expressing the law of progress thus indicated, which, whatever be its value, seems to me to be suf-
ficiently ascertained. All the forms of Status taken notice of
in the Law of Persons were derived from, and to some ex-
tent are still colored by, the powers and privileges ancient-
ly residing in the Family. If then we employ Status, agree-
able with the usage of the best writers, to signify these per-
sonal conditions only, and avoid applying the term to such
conditions as are the immediate or remote result of agreement, we may say that the movement of the progressive societies has hitherto been a movement from Status to Contract." (Maine, 1873:164-65).

2

The usage of the concept in Maine, then, would appear to correspond very roughly to what the modern social scientist would call "ascribed status." No such limitation is placed on the concept by Max Radin (1934:373): "Status is essentially a legal term and connotes the sum of the legal capacities of an individual, his powers to enforce legal rights and obligations either for himself or for others." That Radin does not differentiate status from contract definitionally seems clear when he asserts the possibility of voluntary status, although it must be noted that he is still within Maine's definition in referring this to marriage, or more broadly to kinship: "Certain complexes of rights, obligations and privileges determined by present law exist of course, but the acquisition of such complexes is voluntary. Thus a marital relationship affects the legal position of the parties in private law, and there is accordingly a status of being married. Those who assume the status, however, do so voluntarily." (Radin, 1934:377).

In a definition which has become anthropologically classic, Linton (1936:113) follows the legal definition to a degree in treating the status of an individual: "However, unless the term is qualified in some way, the status of any individual means the sum total of all the statuses which he occupies. It represents his position with relation to the total society." The broadening of the term in social science is made quite explicit in Linton's definition of generic status (1936:113): "A status, as distinct from the individual who may occupy it, is simply a collection of rights and duties." Linton's generic use of the concept is clear from the fact that he goes on to differentiate between ascribed and achieved status. There is no attempt to distinguish positions based on contract from those based on kinship. Equally abstract and generalizing is Parsons' definition. Speaking of the participation of the individual actor in the social system, Parsons (1951:25) says: "This participation in turn has two principal aspects. On the one hand there is the positional aspect-- that of where the actor in question is 'located' in the social system relative to other actors. This is what we will call his status, which is his place in the relationship system considered as a structure, that is a patterned system of parts."

The conception of status as a position in a pattern clearly implies that the pattern is one of rights and duties; thus, while undergoing considerable change in definition in moving

3

from law to social science, the concept of status has retained the core of its original legal meaning. The term has been broadened by the exclusion of contract as a definitional criterion. It has been additionally broadened by extension beyond the field of those rights and duties defined by strictly legal precedent, to include those which are part of formal custom, a step which is necessary to place the comparison between "primitive" and "civilized" societies on a firm footing.

A final clarification of the term status should be made. It has become popular to use the term to signify hierarchical position to the exclusion of other types of social position, especially in common speech. The differentiation is nicely made by Warner and Lunt (1942:3): "The term 'rank' refers here to series of higher and lower statuses or positions; the term 'status' is a more general word which applies to any social position and does not necessarily refer to high and lower ranking." This usage will be followed in this study.

An outstanding, if inexplicit, feature of the anthropological treatment of status is the terminological method, a method made necessary by the ethnographer's position as interpreter of strange societies to Europeans in European languages. A terminological approach to status is implicit in most ethnographic work, but it is unavoidable when one is confronted with native status terms for which there are no precise equivalents in European status systems. The confusion over proper usage of "priest" or "curer" or "magician" is illustrative of the difficulty. It has proved convenient in many cases simply to conserve the native terms for the more untranslatable statuses, and to report the foreign society in its own language. The Zuni koyemshi, the Eskimo angakok, the Ifugao monkalun, the Yaqui pascola, the Narragansett sachem, the Tungus shaman, are familiar examples. In some cases the identification of native status terms has been made in free translation; rather than seek corresponding European statuses, the ethnographer has elected to give us the connotations of the native term or to create specialized terminology. Such expressions as "crazy dog," "cross cousin," "sibling of opposite sex," "clan brother," "ceremonial friend," "manly hearted women," "age mate," "kula partner," "seal inviter," or "singer" exemplify this process. The problems of translation are more difficult in some areas of social life than in others; the technological statuses, for

4

example, are rarely given in the native language, while ceremonial organization is particularly difficult to analogize from culture to culture.

The most explicit and systematic application of the terminological method, however, has been in that peculiarly anthropological pastime, the study of kinship terminologies. Here the first discovery may be credited to Morgan, whose Systems of Consanguinity and Affinity (1870) demonstrates the first real awareness of the configurational differences between systems of kinship terms. Spier's Kinship Systems of North America (1925) summarizes the considerable body of data which consistent anthropological interest in the idea had brought together for this continent by 1925. Although in time many questions were raised about the degree to which status terms in fact reflect actual behavior, the anthropological interest has persisted and has been vindicated in such achievements as Murdock's Social Structure (1949), a work which builds directly upon long years of consistent professional interest in this field. Lévi-Strauss (1949) has more recently added to the impressive anthropological theory of kinship structure the hypothesis that it may operate essentially as an exchange system (L.-S., 1949), and that it may parallel basic linguistic structure (L.-S., 1951), and there are other indications that we have not reached the end of this rich vein. Of the many factors which have doubtless contributed to the anthropological success in this line of theory, we may elect to emphasize one: kinship analysis rests firmly on the assumption of the single status as its fundamental unit of analysis.

A method so fruitful in one field of social organization study would seem to merit serious consideration in relation to others. Despite certain important theoretical difficulties, the collection of status terminologies in the area of kinship has given to the field of social anthropology a method which is peculiarly its own and has proved singularly successful. It is important to recognize the limitations of the method. Phenomenal status, as indicated by the existence of a native term for a particular social position, does not necessarily cover all forms of interaction in a given society, but it should prove to be an accurate reflection of all those forms of interaction of which the people of the society are explicitly aware. Thus the kinship system may not distinguish birth order of siblings even though birth order of siblings is in

5

some sense important. Presumably, however, there can be no explicit rules governing the behavior of siblings differentiated by birth order unless there is a term which enables the individual to make such a differentiation more or less easily. Starting from the native terminology of status enables us to treat the phenomenon of status from the point of view of the native informant. One need hardly say that this does not preclude analysis from the viewpoint of the observer.

These and other considerations which will emerge later lead to proposal of the following definition of a status term: a status term is a word designating a class of individuals occupying (simultaneously or serially) a single position in the social system, with specific defining patterns of rights and duties, the fulfillment of which is legitimized and guaranteed by sanctions. The use of this definition in the light of the preceding discussion should make possible the collection of status terminologies representative not only of the area of kinship but of the entire social system of a given culture.

The terminological approach to entire status systems has certain hypothetical advantages which it is the purpose of this paper to explore. It gives us a comprehensive view of the total society. The collection of terminologies can be exhaustive. The method is objective while simultaneously giving us a view of the society from the standpoint of the people living in it; it is objectively subjective. It provides us with a "natural unit" for further analysis of social organization, of which the analysis of social complexity later in this paper is one example. It makes possible a configurational view of the social system and a structural analytic framework for descriptive and comparative purposes, rendering both description and comparison more systematic. Finally, it may serve as a springboard to a wide range of problems in the study of social organization, demography, social change, social psychology, institutional sociology and stratification.

In order to test the utility of this method and to explore the problems attendant upon such research, we have attempted to gather together the complete status terminologies of nine aboriginal cultures of North America. It has seemed essential to select systems of a convenient simplicity, and the North American Indian societies present us with this advantage. The cultures were selected so as to be representative of the nine culture areas into which Kroeber (1939) di-

6

vides the continent north of Mexico. No attempt was made to select cultures at random, since this type of research requires that the available ethnographic materials be as complete as possible. Accordingly, the cultures selected are among the best known cultures on the continent. The "cultures" were isolated primarily on a linguistic basis, the assumption being that a group with a common, mutually intelligible language would share a common system of status terminology. Except in the case of a few terms, dialectic differentiation did not appear to present any major problems.

The cultures selected were: (1) for the Arctic, the Central-Greenlandic Eskimo ca. 1900; (2) for the Northwest Coast, the Kwakiutl ca. 1880; (3) for the Northwest Interior, the Chipewyan ca. 1900, including the related dialects of Chipewyan, Slave, Yellowknife, and Caribou-Eater; (4) for California, the Yokuts ca. 1800; (5) for the Basin, the Shoshone ca. 1840, including the related dialects of Eastern Shoshone, Gosiute, Western Shoshone, and Comanche; (6) for the Southwest, the Zuni ca. 1600; (7) for the Plains, the Sioux ca. 1870, including the Assiniboine, Yanktonai, Yankton, and Teton Dakota; (8) for the Woodlands, the Algonkin ca. 1800, including Algonkin, Ojibway, Ottawa, and Missisauga; (9) for the Southeast, the Choctaw ca. 1700, including the closely related Chickasaw. The dates given are approximations to the "ethnographic present" represented in the collated data.

The Chipewyan sources used were Honigmann (1946 and 1949) and Mason (1946). The Eskimo data are drawn from Boas (1888), Rasmussen (1931), and Stefansson (1919). The Zuni sources were Bunzel (1932a and 1932b), Eggan (1950), Kroeber (1917), Parsons (1933), and Stevenson (1904). The Yokuts sources were Gayton (1930 and 1948), Kroeber (1925), and Newman (1944). The Sioux materials are from Hassrick (1944), Lowie (1909 and 1913), Walker (1917), and Wissler (1912). The sources for the Algonkin were Brown (1952), Jenness (1935), Landes (1937), Skinner (1911 and 1914), and Speck (1915). The Kwakiutl references consulted were Boas (1897, 1921, 1925, and 1930), and the Shoshone data were drawn from Gladwin (1948), Hoebel (1939 and 1940), Lowie (1915), and Steward (1938). Sources used for the Choctaw data were Bushnell (1909), Byington (1915), Eggan (1937), and Swanton (1911, 1918, and 1931).

In surveying the literature on these nine cultures the im-

7

plications of the definition of status terms given above have been followed. We have noted wherever possible the native term given in the ethnographic reports for all social positions where sanction-supported privileges and obligations were described or implied. In many cases we have also noted the English term for a position which seemed to meet the same criteria and where the implication of the ethnographer seemed to be that a native term existed even though he did not cite it. The collection of the complete systems proved more difficult than was anticipated, and in some cases contradictions between sources have been somewhat arbitrarily resolved. For ease of transcription the phonetic recordings of native terms in the various languages were simplified wherever this could be done without obviously violating phonemic principles, and simpler symbols were substituted for those involving diacritical marks.

Because important matters of judgment are involved at many points in the compilation, collation, and assessment of the American Indian status terms, it has been deemed necessary to present the terminologies in some detail (see Appendix). The specialist will be able to judge the adequacy with which various of the societies are represented by the terms reported, and the general reader will perhaps gain a sense of the rich complexity inherent in even the simplest assemblage of terms from some of the world's "simpler" cultures.

In presenting the terminological data it is convenient to distinguish three main types of statuses, differentiable on structural and taxonomic grounds: (1) ascribed status, (2) achieved status, and (3) associational status. Ascribed status, including age, sex, and kinship statuses, based as it is upon biological principles elevated to sociological significance, includes a terminology so well defined and so precisely analytic that we are aware of a sharp upper limit to the number of terms which would be possible in this area. Furthermore, this limit is probably approached as closely by the world's simplest cultures (e.g., the superprimitive Australians) as by its most complex. It is even conceivable, indeed, that elaboration of other areas of social structure may have an inverse relationship to the elaboration of ascribed statuses.

Achieved status, here considered to include religious, economic, and political terminology, is subject to no such

8

limits. New inventions of technology, ideology, or social form and the quasi-evolutionary self-complication of social systems as they develop progressively through time result in elaboration and multiplication of statuses in this area to a degree not even theoretically possible in age, sex, and kinship terminologies. Nevertheless, though we may be unable to set precise quantitative limits to this elaboration, it seems quite likely that limits do exist and that mutually interactive demographic, ideological, and ecological factors have an impact upon status structure explicable, if somewhat crudely, in terms of stages in a process of social evolution. In another sense, these "stages" must be interpreted of course against the background of the culture-historical position of a given society, and the availability to it, through invention and diffusion, of the elements which underlie status differentiation.

In order to handle the problem of status differentiation and social complexity, it has been necessary for us to consider associational structure as separate from the foregoing types. This is so because the elaboration of associational memberships is not dependent upon limited principles of human biology or even upon the cumulative and progressive causation of achieved status differentiation in any simple sense. The formation of associations is dependent upon the legal fiction of corporate entities; hence, theoretically, the number of associations in a society may be indefinitely multiplied by simple reduplication. If, however, as is frequently the case, the associations expand through creation of new groupings which, though distinct and exclusive, are identical structurally with the existing units, the net effect is the segmentation or fracturing of the society and the creation in effect of a number of subsocieties. We must insist, therefore, that, as our definition of a status terms implies, not all terms denote statuses, even though we are proceding on the assumption that all statuses will be named.

It will perhaps seem confusing initially that we treat as associations not only voluntary organizations, such as the dance societies, ceremonial associations, fraternities, orders, and moieties of the Indian societies, but also such units as clans and gentes, phratries, bands, villages, tribes, age grades, and ranks. Our reason for so doing is that, regardless of the point at which these groupings articulate with the ascribed and achieved status systems, their struc-

9

ture is different from the structure of those systems. Although empirically the complications of associational structure are not infinite, it seems impossible to place any theoretical limit on the possible elaboration of them. The Indian systems only dimly foreshadow the highly differentiated associational systems of the more complex of contemporary cultures; still they warn us of the nature of this differentiation. It is crucial to note that not only are associations different from achieved and ascribed status in structure, but that they constitute a homogeneous class of social forms as well. One need but point to the empirical interchangeability of kinship, residential, ceremonial, political, occupational, age, and sex groupings. We have great difficulty, in fact, determining limits between these types. In historic cases tribes may become castes (as in India), bands become clans (Navaho), ceremonial associations become age-graded (as among the Sioux), and age grades become sex-differentiated (Kwakiutl), bands take on political significance and become tribal (Shoshone), and priesthoods become generic ranks (Choctaw). This flexibility of form, absolutely out of the question in ascribed status and rare with respect to achieved statuses, is the essence of the associational form of organization, following from the quasi-individual treatment of associations as corporate bodies.

2. Ascribed Status

THE ASCRIBED STATUSES are those defined in terms of biological characteristics. Since the number of such characteristics used in known social systems is sharply limited, it is convenient to survey ascribed statuses analytically in terms of a few general structuring criteria. The primary determinants of these are age, sex, mating, generation (or birth) and death, and their derivatives. Secondary determinants which stand out in the terminologies include generalization of terms, the appearance of defective systems, the appearance of alternative systems, extension of terms, reciprocity, absolute and relative reference, and relation of terms to speaker or referent. In a few cases there is inclusion of specific status within generic statuses. It is convenient to start by distinguishing six areas of ascribed status, each of which will be presented separately: (1) age-sex terminology, (2) nuclear kinship, (3) lineal kinship, (4) collateral kinship, (5) affinal kinship, and (6) decedent kinship.

Age-Sex Terminology

A caveat should be entered with regard to the terminologies of age and sex. Although these are often reported in the ethnographic literature, the presentation is frequently casual and rarely inspires confidence in the completeness of the reporting. In this area, therefore, we are proceeding on hints and hunches and the analysis may be subject to extensive revision.

It is noteworthy nonetheless that the systems do display differences, and it is perhaps relevant to the question of the reliability of the reporting that none of the terminologies appears to be identical with the pattern in English. The number of age-sex status terms ranges from nine to eighteen.

A number of common features do appear. Every system implies the assumption of sexlessness of infants, and although the exact age at which the attribute of sex becomes socially relevant appears to vary, every system begins this differentiation at some point in childhood and extends it systematically to old age. Four of the systems (Shoshone, Zuni, Yokuts, and Sioux) have the berdache; the remaining five do not. Impressionistically, one may add that the critical points for differentiating statuses also seem to be constant, though some of them are glossed over in some cultures; birth, suckling, weaning, language and locomotion, puberty, maturity, aging, senility, and death.

Nuclear Kinship

Even in the area of kinship in the first degree, there is considerable variation among the systems. Purely quantitatively the range is from 11 to 31 terms. Common elements shared by all nine groups are terms for father, mother, son, daughter, husband, and wife and some differentiation of siblings by relative age. Differences among the systems include the presence or absence of neuter terms ("parent," "child," "spouse," or "sibling"), differentiation of siblings by "sex of speaker," spouse terms derivative of polygamy, and child terms differentiated by birth order. Partial alternative usages exist in several languages for "sibling," and complete sets of alternative sibling terms are found in Algonkin and Kwakiutl.

Lineal Kinship

Kinship in the second degree in the second ascending and descending generation appears to be somewhat less variable. The number of terms varies from three to ten, the higher number resulting from inclusion of more distant relational terms for lineally ascending and descending relatives of the third and fourth generations. Various forms of reciprocal terminology are common but not universal in the sample, and there are some unusual terminological generalizations. (The Chipewyan equation of younger brother with grandson is

12

an example.) No single type of term is found in all nine systems in this area.

Collateral Kinship

Terms for parents' siblings, siblings' children, and cousins are perhaps the most variable in the framework of kinship. The systems range from five to 14 terms, and no single differentiation is found in all nine systems. Alternative terms or sets of terms are common; reciprocals are frequent; the sex of speaker and of intervening relatives are differentia as often as the sex of the referent. There are, in fact, few problems of kinship terminology not represented in the collateral terminology for these nine groups. In view of the attention paid to the collection and analysis of the terminology of collateral kinship it seems remarkable that the data remain incomplete or ambiguous in almost every case.

Affinal Kinship

No particular type of affinal term is common to the nine cultures in the sample. Terms specific to this area of kinship range from one to 21 in number, the elaborate Shoshone system being worthy of special comment. The ethnographic coverage of this area of kinship is incomplete, since some systems yield specific terms for grandparental in-laws or affinal uncles and aunts, the absence of which would not ordinarily be explicitly noted.

Decedent Kinship

The terminologies for American Indian cultures are rarely complete with respect to the relationships brought about by death of a relative or by death and remarriage. The structure of those compiled here, furthermore, is so similar to English as to inspire _ipso_ _facto_ at least a mild suspicion. The Choctaw terminology appears to be complete, but the remainder are so fragmentary that they must be considered as scarcely more than guesses.

Other Ascribed Statuses

A variety of additional terms was collected for one of the

13

cultures or another which refer to marital status (marriageable, bachelor, newlywed, etc.), aspects of birth (twin, pregnant, barren, etc.), and extended or distant kinship (ancestor, relative, etc.). Terms for ceremonial kinship and extended kin groups are treated elsewhere. Since these terms are very sketchily reported they are simply reported as a residuum in order to make the total list as complete as possible, but failure to include a Zuni term for "twin" or a Shoshone term for "distant relative" must not be interpreted as indicating that such terms do not exist. We have refrained from assuming their existence when evidence was lacking.

A cursory review of the structure of the terminologies of ascribed status for these nine American Indian societies will show that no two of the systems are exactly alike. Still the frequent identity of elements or groups of elements from system to system gives us a basis for comparing them. We may perhaps state briefly the common elements and then describe the more salient anomalies of these nine societies. All nine of them apparently distinguish at least five age levels: all have at least one neuter status covering infancy and at least four sex-differentiated terms for the subsequent age statuses. All have sex-differentiated terms for parent, child, and spouse, and all recognize relative age plus at least one sex-differentiating criterion of sibling status. All of them differentiate grandparents' and parents' siblings by sex of reference. Furthermore, all nine societies distinguish the kinship statuses named so far from each other, even though they are not always differentiated from certain others; thus, the common minimal ascribed status structure of the nine Indian societies includes twenty-three analytic positions, roughly describable as: infant, boy, girl, young man, young woman, adult man, adult woman, old man, old woman, father, mother, son, daughter, husband, wife, older brother, older sister, younger brother, younger sister, uncle, aunt, grandfather, and grandmother.

There are several ways in which the remaining areas of kinship manifest their dependency upon the fourteen kinship statuses in this list, and their more variable definition from culture to culture. Outside this core area the systems may be defective: the terms may simply be lacking. When this occurs, the slack is taken up by generalization: a neighboring or related term is stretched to cover the blank spot. The commonest form of generalization is the overriding of sex

14

difference illustrated in the neuter terms ("grandchild," for example, in place of "grandson" and "granddaughter"). A more complex example is the Sioux hunkasi (parallel cousin), which reduces the complex sixteen-term structure of Siouan cousin terminology by half at one stroke, overriding the distinctions in sex of referent, speaker, and intervening relative, which are manifested in the other half of the terminology. Generalization is also the process whereby terms are extended from the basic statuses named above to other areas of kinship. Thirteen forms of this order of generalization occur in our sample: parent terms are extended to spouse's parent, step-parent, or cousin (this last is in "Crow-Omaha-type" kinship); child terms are extended to sibling's child, grandchild, child's spouse, and stepchild; sibling terms are extended to cousin, grandchild, sibling-in-law, and step- or half-siblings; grandparent terms are extended to grandchild; and parent's sibling terms are extended to cousin (again the Crow or Omaha case). The only form of generalization common elsewhere which does not appear in our data is the equation of parent's sibling with parent. The spouse terms appear never to generalize.

The existence of alternative systems is a complicating factor in our data. It is worthy of note, however, that the phenomenon is of limited occurrence. Our data furnish eleven examples: alternative sibling terms for the Kwakiutl and Algonkin; lineal terminologies for the Yokuts and Zuni; nephew-niece terms for the Yokuts and Algonkin; cousin terms for the Shoshone and Algonkin; parent-in-law terms for the Shoshone; and grandparent terms for the Sioux. The final example, the alternative Sioux child terminology, is especially elaborate and anomalous; it is probably not a true alternative system in usage. It seems likely that, in general, the alternative systems are symptoms of terminological change; however, their very existence is in some cases inferential, with the result that it is difficult to generalize.

A further problem which occurs in the terminologies is that of reciprocality of terms. Complete terminological reciprocals (see Kroeber, 1917, for a discussion of reciprocality), in which A calls B and only B "x" and B calls A and only A "x," occur in all the systems but Zuni's. The English "cousin" may be taken as an example. A complete list of the examples for the nine American Indian societies follows:

Kwakiutl: sibsamesex-sibsamesex
             siboppsex-siboppsex
             hasibsamesex-hasibsamesex
             hasiboppsex-hasiboppsex
             sppa-chsp
             spgrpa-grchsp

Yokuts: momo-wodach
             famo-wosoch
             copainlaw-copainlaw
             husi-wobrwi
             wibr-masihu

Shoshone: cooppsex-cooppsex
             fafa-masoch
             famo-wosoch
             mofa-madach
             momo-wodach
             grgrpa-grgrch
             grgrgrpa-grgrgrch
             fabr-mabrch
             fasi-wobrch
             mobr-masich
             mosi-wosich
             mamaleco-mamaleco
             wofemaleco-wofemaleco
             sibinlawoppsex-sibinlawoppsex
             masihu-wibr
             wobrwi-husi

Algonkin: mabr-mabr
             wosi-wosi
             siboppsex-siboppsex
             crosscooppsex-crosscooppsex
             copainlaw-copainlaw
             masihu-wibr
             wobrwi-husi
             sibinlawoppsex-sibinlawoppsex

Eskimo: sib-sib

Sioux: parallelco-parallelco

Chipewyan:	sibinlaw-sibinlaw
Choctaw:	sppa-chsp

Reliable data on the more extended relationships proved scattered; great-aunts and -uncles, great-grandparents, and similarly distant relatives were not covered in most of the systems. These and other similar relationships furnish the primary materials for the most distinctive variations in terminology. Special terms were noted in Yokuts, for example, for spouse's sibling's spouse. The existence of terms for the third, fourth and/or fifth generations of lineal relatives has been noted for the Kwakiutl, Shoshone, and Zuni. Special terms were also found for "co-wife" in Chipewyan and Algonkin and for "second wife" in Choctaw, and Algonkin also has a distinctive term for "widow of a gens brother." A Kwakiutl term of some interest is one referring specifically to "parent's cousin." It is in Sioux, however, that the most remarkable concentration of distinctive terms occurs. A full set of terms differentiating the relative age of offspring and an additional term for "favorite son" in Sioux are probably indicative of a Siouan value premise. Equally remarkable are the specialized Sioux terms for spouse: "polygynous husband," "sororal plural wife," "nonsororal plural wife," "captured wife," and "wife of consummated marriage." Aside from the Sioux terms, we can rarely be sure that these "specialized" or anomalous terms are actually lacking in the systems for which we have not reported them. Complete and reliable data here, as in the area of the "miscellaneous" terms previously reported, would probably do much to illuminate the structure of ascribed status.

17

3. Achieved Status

THE FUNDAMENTAL definitions of achieved statuses differ, of course, from those of ascribed statuses. The latter involve many things but are defined in terms of a scant few: age, sex, birth, mating, and death. Achieved statuses may also involve these factors, but their definitions must be stated in terms not of biology but of the behavior expected from a person in this or that position in society: the definitions are definitions not of attribute but of action. The primary mechanism for multiplication of achieved statuses would seem to be the division of labor. This results not only in a differentiation of a number of generic statuses, but often also in the subdivision of these statuses into more specific substatuses, differentiated from the generic status only by specificity. Thus, for example, any Kwakiutl shaman is called paxala; he may be a thrower shaman, sucking shaman, dream shaman, etc., but all of the more specific terms imply the applicability of the generic term. Generic statuses are defined as mutually exclusive; substatuses, mutually exclusive in relation to each other, are explicitly included in a more general term. Much of the multiplication of terminology in the Indian systems is by substatus differentiation.

In order to specify the precise way in which status systems differentiate their various component positions, we must have a set of concepts categorizing the action definitions of statuses. It seems useful to start by differentiating these definitions according to the object of the action: (1) human, (2) natural, and (3) supernatural. Our classification must be based upon the status definitions as the people of

the culture see them (mediated, of course, by the ethnographer's English translation and explanations). The trichotomy
proposed is consistent with Malinowski's assertion that
primitive peoples are able to and invariably do make these
distinctions even though their thought may appear animistic
or illogical to people of another culture. In broad terms
this classification enables us to differentiate the areas of
political, economic, and religious structure. It is worth
noting in this connection that any status definition which includes man as the object of action implies an object status
for such a man to occupy.

Finally, we may introduce various categories descriptive
of the mode of the action which defines the status. These include such assumptions as that the subject of action or occupant of the status (1) communicates (information, orders,
etc.) to the object, (2) has physical or quasi-physical (mag-
ical) power over the object in the sense of ability to alter it,
or (3) owns the object. In relation to social structure these
categories are assumed to be universal and fundamental. A
given system may differentiate many positions through the
application of more detailed sets of categories (specific
techniques of supernatural communication or specific types
of power or ownership), but as far as this framework goes
it seems to cover comparable aspects of social structure
well enough to make possible a comparative analysis.

Religious Terminology

The various permutations of these fundamental categories
provide us with a basis for comparison of systems. Thus
we may distinguish those cases in which the definition of the
status is in terms of power over, communication with, or
ownership of the supernatural as the area of religious statuses.

Magical

The nine cultures studied have from two to fifteen differentiated statuses defined in terms of power over a supernatural object. Shamanism, witchcraft, curing, burial, and
weather control seem to be the primary foci of these relationships. In all cases these statuses are those in which the

19

individual is manipulating the supernatural in a ritual attempt to control it for human ends.

The systems vary in complexity and structure from the simple two-term (shaman/witch) system of the Chipewyan to the rather highly organized medicomagical system of the Choctaw. There is a general emphasis on shamanism (all but Zuni) and a general differentiation of the beneficial magic of the shaman from witchcraft (all but Sioux). Status differentiation of curing from other aspects of shamanism occurs only in the more complex cultures (Algonkin, Choctaw, Kwakiutl, and Zuni), and the professionalization of ritual for the benefit of the whole society, such as food supply or weather control, emerges in almost the same cases (Choctaw, Kwakiutl, and Zuni), though it may be fore-shadowed in the Algonkin "leader" of Mide ritual or the "jimsonweed leader" of the Yokuts and similar statuses. Specific recognition of the status of funeral manager characterizes the Yokuts, Algonkin, and Choctaw, but the lack of such a term for the other "complex societies" may be only a lack of data. Finally, at least two societies (Shoshone and Kwakiutl) explicitly recognize the status of novice; again it seems unlikely that some similar provision would not be made at least in those cultures with a highly complex shamanism (Choctaw) or ritual system (Zuni). The terms may simply have been overlooked.

Oracular Terminology

The second general area of religious organization comprises those statuses which involve communication with the supernatural. Prophecy, divining, prayer, and at least some of the ritual song of the American Indians would fall in this sphere. Some form of communication with the supernatural is also a fundamental and undifferentiated part of shamanism, and is part of the religious conception of the Indians in ways unlinked to differentiated statuses (as in the vision, dream, or nonprofessional interpretation of signs and omens). Somewhat arbitrarily, in the absence of any very explicit data to the contrary, we have omitted nonlinguistic communication from this area and have classified ritual drumming and dancing elsewhere. The statuses which are developed in this area for the American Indian cultures are two: prophet and singer. For the Algonkin the prophet is differentiated into seer and diviner. For the Yokuts, the singer is differentiated from the songmaker. The Kwakiutl seer has been equated with prophet. The lack of Algonkin and Choctaw terms for singer seems improbable but the terms were not discovered.

Fetishistic Terminology

In the area of ownership of the supernatural, American Indian social structures are unspecific. The widespread idea of a guardian spirit coupled with vision quest or other avenues to supernatural power are largely left without formal recognition in terms of status. Ownership of supernatural paraphernalia or of artifacts used in ritual seems to be largely an aspect of statuses otherwise defined. Three terms seem to belong inescapably in the category of ownership of the supernatural: the Sioux drumkeeper (native term not discovered), the Kwakiutl mamanats'enox (drumkeeper), and the Zuni fetish guardian (native term not discovered). It should be mentioned, of course, that shamanism often involves the idea of individual ownership of "power" which may be transferred from person to person in exactly the same manner as other property, but this remains unelaborated in terms of status.

Economic Terminology

The economic area of social structure may be set apart conceptually as referring to those statuses defined in terms of man's relationship to nature: the statuses designate persons who have power over nature, ownership of natural phenomena, or an identification with nature. The fourth logical possibility, that of communication with nature, is eliminated here on grounds that this is by definition a supernatural category, and the statuses which might have been technically described as referring to communication with nature are dealt with under communication with the supernatural. Trade or economic exchange have been subsumed under the rubric of "property."

Despite a wealth of information about the technology of the North American Indian, we have very few descriptions of how their technologies were organized into status systems. Upon examination of the ethnographies one comes to the conclusion that this is at least partially the result of a genuine simplicity of structure. Many of the structures are, indeed, so schematic that they scarcely command the attention of the ethnographer, who becomes necessarily more preoccupied with the far more difficult problems of ritual systems or of associational organization. The technology of the American Indians north of Mexico was simple, and their economic structure was by and large even simpler. We must of course reserve judgment on whether the mere presence of pottery making as a cultural trait implies the status of potter, although it seems reasonable that no very intricate ceramic tradition can be built up without the degree of specialization which requires a special term and status definition. The number of status terms in the Indian economic systems is certainly much smaller than the number of economic techniques the Indians are known to have possessed. Still the lack of explicit attention to this aspect of social structure by many of the ethnographers casts some doubt upon the completeness of the terminologies collected. The safest procedure seems to be to accept as status terms only those which seem to fit a rigorous application of the definition. Whether additional terms might be added in some or all of the systems remains a question to be answered by further data.

Technological Terminology

Among the statuses defined in terms of power over nature, only one is present in all nine of the cultures in our sample: that of hunter. The progressive differentiation of other statuses is primarily in terms of technique and the natural object of the technique. Fishing is given occasional recognition in this way; gathering techniques are infrequently identified, and agricultural occupations are distinguished in the two cultures (Choctaw and Zuni) with a highly developed agriculture. Handicraft statuses are given progressive recognition in the more complex systems and appear to correlate in a general way with other aspects of increasing structural complexity. To continue the example cited above, potter is a status reliably reported only for the Choctaw and the Zuni, although many of the other groups had pottery. A special problem in taxonomy is presented by the statuses of curer, herbalist, doctor, and midwife, reported for many of the cultures. It is not always clear whether these statuses are defined in natural or supernatural terms, and it is likely that in at least some cases both elements are involved. Although they have been primarily assigned to the supernatural category, these positions are relisted in the economic structure as well, as a matter of perspective. A final special problem is presented by the musician status (principally the American Indian drummer). Somewhat arbitrarily we have included this position in the economic structure despite the clearly ceremonial context of the drummer's action because of the lack of any explicitly supernatural rationale for the drummer's activity. Drumming seems to be neither a supernatural power technique (as is juggling), nor a supernatural communicative technique (as is singing), nor yet a human communicative technique (as is African drumming). Accordingly, we have fallen back upon the activity definition itself and classified drumming as a status defined by power over ("physical action upon") nature.

Terminology of Property

A separable part of the system of economic statuses is that concerned with ownership and manipulation of property, or the ownership of nature. In the American Indian sample, four of the systems (Chipewyan, Shoshone, Algonkin, and Sioux) yielded no terms which are defined in this way. In the remaining five cultures, the terms discovered seem to refer primarily to broad categories of ownership comparable to socioeconomic class (rich, poor, noble, commoner, etc.), to modes of transfer of title or the manipulation of property (trader, auctioneer, gambler), or to specific property rights possibly including the rights to human labor (house owner, boat owner, laborer, worker, etc.). The ethnographic data tend to be somewhat nonspecific about some of these categories. Furthermore, in many of the cultures property rights may not define a special status but simply operate as part of statuses otherwise defined. This is true, for example, of the Eskimo steersman or the Algonkin hunter, who have very specific property rights to game or to a game preserve. The full analysis of such statuses becomes a matter for quite detailed treatment, and we have preferred to avoid these more specialized problems in this study.

Although class stratification has never been noted as a primary feature of the Eskimo social system, the reliable account of a class type of differentiation holds considerable theoretical interest and has therefore been included among the Eskimo terms in the sample. The differentiation is based terminologically upon ownership of the most important single capital investment in Eskimo technology--boats. The intent of the terms seems to be the differentiation of the well-to-do umialik who owns an umiak or large boat (and presumably has a considerable variety of lesser capital goods as well-- kayak, sled, dog team, and household equipment), and the destitute ilialuk who does not even own a kayak and lacks the resources for properly caring for a family. As described, the system would seem to imply a middle term for the Eskimos with adequate but unspectacular equipment for hunting and travel, but no such term is reported. It is interesting that this set of terms is reported for the Eskimo but not for such groups as the Sioux and Algonkin. Presumably the explanation would relate to the relatively substantial investment which the Eskimo makes in his specialized technological equipment as compared with other hunting peoples.

The Yokuts constitute something of a problem in connection with property categories. Such terms as are reported suggest a system rather closely parallel to that of the Choctaw and Zuni, and one is strongly tempted to assume the existence of terms (or statuses) which are not explicitly reported in the Yokuts ethnographies. The possible existence of a term for trader suggests that the importance of trade among the Yokuts may have been analogous to that among the Choctaw, Zuni, and Kwakiutl. The existence of a special and somewhat problematic term for worker or laborer in the same four cultures (and no others) also suggests fundamental structural similarity. Class terms, however, are not reported for the Yokuts. The Choctaw system apparently differentiates at least three class levels: the nobility (including chiefs and the members of the military-religious orders), laborers (?), and the poor. As in all the Indian cultures except Eskimo, one might add slaves as the fourth and lowest stratum of society, but it seems simpler to deal with slavery separately. In addition to the class terminology, Choctaw distinguishes the status of trader, and also that of gambler. Somewhat arbitrarily the latter status has been classified as a special case of manipulation of property, but its structural importance is open to question.

The Zuni system is quite similar to the Choctaw with the noteworthy exception that whereas rank is the fundamental

validation of upper-class status in Choctaw society, Zuni emphasizes supernatural "wealth" and plays down the element of rank. The terminologies, however, are quite parallel. Zuni terms exist for rich, laborer, and poor, and there are special terms for trader and auctioneer. The Kwakiutl system elaborates the rank principle far more than any of the other cultures in the sample, although the exact terms of the Kwakiutl system are somewhat confusing and the number of ranked levels is not clear. The importance of ownership categories for the Kwakiutl is emphasized by the existence of a special term designating a man who has had property but has retired from its management. The term for trader, rather vaguely indicated in the ethnographic descriptions of the Kwakiutl, almost certainly existed. The Northwest Coast is known to have been an area of active trading of a more than casual sort.

Political Terminology

In the political area of social structure we are dealing with the social statuses defined in terms of action with man as an object. To put the argument in more familiar language the political modality is that in which man exercises conscious and formal control over the actions of other men. Th types of status categories with which we are concerned are those of power over (physical action upon) man, communica tion with man, and ownership of man. Thus we are concerned with the statuses of warfare and other forms of coe cion, authority and command, and slavery. As has alread been noted, the statuses in this area, being defined in ter of action upon a human object, imply a status which is the object of the action. This relationship may be simple as the case of master and slave, or warrior and enemy, or be organized into complex chains of hierarchical comma as in the rank system of a modern army, or into even m complex systems of partly hierarchical, partly correla statuses as in the Zuni "theocratic" political structure.

Terminology of Force

In connection with statuses defined in terms of powe man, restricting this term to the use of physical (or i cal) force, the American Indian systems are quite si

and the resulting statuses are of two types: warrior and police. The former is found in all nine of the cultures, and includes the substatus scout (guard or watchman) in the Shoshone, Algonkin, Sioux, Choctaw, and Kwakiutl systems. The differentiation of a specialized police status, variously identified with the ceremonial clown or outstanding performance in war, is reliably indicated for the Shoshone, Algonkin, Sioux, and Zuni. In general, the object status for warrior is enemy; for scout it is the same; for police it is vaguely "the people," no distinctions being made for rank and station.

The lack of terms in the Eskimo and Chipewyan systems is not surprising in view of the established lack of organization or elaboration of warfare among these groups. The lack of terms in Yokuts is of dubious significance. The classification of the Algonkin <u>okichita</u> as a "police" status is impressionistic and based on the apparent diffusion of that term from the Sioux where it clearly signifies police activity both in warfare and in hunting and ceremonial contexts. The lack of terms in Choctaw and Kwakiutl for the police or police-clown status may be due to lack of data. In some cases, notably the Zuni <u>pit'ashiwanni</u> and the Algonkin <u>shimaganish</u>, the warrior terms have an important derivative ceremonial application to particular assistants of the priest or ritual headman. In the Algonkin case warriors may actually have had this additional duty, but at Zuni it seems likely that the ritual "warrior" was completely distinct from the actual fighting men, at least by the time the standard ethnographies were written.

Terminology of Authority

Most authority relationships are structured as statuses in which the primary definition rests upon <u>communication with other human beings</u>. The aim of such communication is assumed to be control of the behavior of the persons towards whom it is directed. It is commonly assumed that such exercise of authority is necessarily a two-way process, in which information goes up the authority hierarchy and orders come down. However, to judge from the American Indian data, the situation is rarely so simple. Hierarchy is, it is true, an outstanding feature of authority structures in all of the groups sampled, yet the data can rarely be described in

the simple terms which would do justice to the "pecking order" dominance of chickens or a herd of cows. Such problems as the coexistence of two or more distinct hierarchies together with the range of difficulties implied (separation of powers, distinction of status occupants, etc.) make it clear that we must have more than a simple hierarchical model to explain human authority systems. The oft-noted American Indian tendency to postpone major decisions until a general consensus is reached is another important factor differentiating all of the Indian authority systems from the more explicit distribution of responsibility and command in European societies.

The American Indian cultures represented in our sample structure their authority systems in four to six more or less distinct hierarchies. The four primary hierarchies found (or probably present) in all nine cultures might be called those of civil, military, religious, and economic authority. In some of the cultures the religious system is split into separate priestly and shamanistic systems, and at Zuni there are at least three different religious systems: the priesthoods, the fraternities, and the kivas. Of special interest from a comparative point of view is the coordinating status of speaker found in all of the systems except Eskimo and Chipewyan, apparently intermediate between the civil and religious systems and involved in both. The only formal machinery for coordination of the systems would seem to be the widespread use of a messenger for communication among the key officials of the separate hierarchies. The assumption which has guided this analysis is that the status definitions of the terms collected are primarily in terms of the other statuses in the same hierarchy. A chief's position is defined primarily in terms of his relationship to the headmen, elders, crier, and people under him. This assumption has been almost inescapable since most of the ethnographers appear to have proceeded on this basis in their descriptions. The result is, however, that the relationship between a chief and a priest, shaman, war leader, or hunt director is not always clear, and the important matters of separation of powers or of spheres of action can only be vaguely indicated. It is probable, especially in the simpler cultures, that a headman very often is also a ritual and military leader; where that is true it is only natural that the status definitions should be vague. The prevalence of such status correspondences in any given culture is, however, an empirical question.

One final explanatory point must be made. Dancer has been classified as a status defined by communication with man, an interpretation which emphasizes the symbolic nature of the dance form while leaving the distinction between verbal and nonverbal communication open to further study. The inclusion of dancers in the context of what might otherwise be considered purely "authority structure" is necessarily arbitrary in view of the fact that such closely related statuses as singer and drummer have been classified elsewhere. The only defense offered is that the classification seems to fit and to do no major violence to the data. It is possible that a more extensive analysis would make it worthwhile to distinguish as a group the statuses definable in terms of aesthetics.

In interpreting the authority structures as composed of chains of communication, it is useful to distinguish the statuses defined in terms of human communication, and therefore implying an object status, from those defined in terms of action upon the supernatural or upon nature. From the point of view of authority structure, the latter may be thought of as "terminal statuses," that is, it is ultimately the action of the individuals in such positions that is being "controlled" by the authority system. In isolating the separate hierarchies or chains of communication, then, we may think in terms of a chief who makes decisions which are communicated to a headman who makes decisions which are communicated to the elders who make decisions which are communicated to a crier who communicates them to the people who then implement them in action of a ritual or economic order, or in terms of coercive action upon man (warfare). The Indian systems are rarely so precise. Communication is never restricted to these official channels. However, we are concerned with tracing those formal chains of communication which are fundamental to the very definitions of the statuses, and it is inevitable that we present a system which appears more rigid and static than is the case in its actual operation.

The Chipewyan system appears to be defined in terms of four more or less hierarchical chains of communication: the civil (headman-people), religious (shaman-dancer-people), military (war leader-warrior), and economic (hunt

28

leader-hunter) systems. The Eskimo system is identical except for the addition of another ritual (or perhaps recreational) system (narrator-people), the addition of a herald to the civil system (headman-herald-people), and the existence of the masked dancer substatuses. The Shoshone system is fundamentally the same as the Chipewyan but increases the number of levels in the civil system to four (chief-headman-speaker-people) and adds a messenger, apparently for liaison among the "officials" of the separable systems, and a go-between, probably for the settlement of disputes between headmen. The Shoshone system also distinguishes substatuses in the economic sphere in which the differences between hunting and pine-nut gathering and the rabbit surround are recognized.

The Yokuts and Choctaw systems are basically similar. Both share with the preceding systems (and with all of those to follow) the four authority systems of the civil, religious, military, and economic spheres. Both add a "coordinative" system of a speaker who apparently receives instructions from at least the civil and religious (possibly also military and economic) leaders, and who transmits these to the people in formal oratory. This type of system is also characteristic of the societies yet to be described: Algonkin, Sioux, Kwakiutl, and Zuni. Like the Shoshone, the Choctaw and Yokuts have the liaison status of messenger, which they also share with the Kwakiutl and Zuni. (The Algonkin and Sioux systems may be small and simple enough that such a status is unnecessary.) The Choctaw, again like the Shoshone, have the special status go-between for management of disputes, an arrangement not found in any of the other systems. In detail the Yokuts system distinguishes five levels in civil authority (chief-headman-elder-crier-people), and at least three in the religious hierarchy (shaman-dancer-people). The position of the shaman-killer is uncertain, and the Yokuts military and economic authority systems are completely in doubt. The Choctaw civil system is at least a four-term system (chief-headman-elder-people), with the interesting additional feature of a special term for chief's wife. The religious system is also a four-term system (high priest-priest-dancer-people), as is the military system (war prophet-officer-warrior-novice). The Choctaw system of economic authority is not specifically reported.

The Sioux and Algonkin systems are so closely parallel as

to approach identity. Both have five "chains of communication": civil, religious, military, economic, and coordinative. Both have a five-term civil system (chief-headman-elder-crier-people). The Sioux religious system has four terms (dance leader-orderly-dancer-people), and the Algonkin system simply multiplies the ritual leader's assistants to six types of "orderly." In the military sphere the systems are identical (war leader-officer-warrior-orderly). The Algonkin economic system is in doubt; the Sioux system involves an elaborate organization for hunting (hunt leader-hunt judge-hunt rationer-hunter).

In addition to the four fundamental systems of authority common to all the tribes, the Kwakiutl and Zuni have the less widespread coordinative and liaison statuses. The Kwakiutl have an additional shamanistic hierarchy distinct from their ceremonial society structure, and Zuni adds a religious society and a _kiva_ system to its priesthood structure. The Kwakiutl system becomes a seven-unit, the Zuni system an eight-unit structure. In the civil authority structure of the Kwakiutl six levels are distinguished (head chief-chief-headman-elder-herald-people), and there are special terms for the chief's wife, son, daughter, and family. The Kwakiutl religious structure is similar to that of the Algonkin and Sioux: (society chief-dancer-attendant-people). The organization of Kwakiutl shamanism involves at least three levels (head shaman-shaman-novice). The structure of military and economic authority among the Kwakiutl is not clear. The liaison status (messenger) in Kwakiutl society is matched by at least two pairs of purely ritual messengers which have been arbitrarily classified as substatuses. The Zuni civil system here reported is in part a Spanish diffusion and involves four levels (chief-assistant chief-crier-people). The "lieutenants" of the chief and assistant chief may be comparable to the "orderlies" or "attendants" of other systems. The Zuni system of religious authority centers on the priesthoods. Approximately six levels of hierarchy may be distinguished: (priest-associate priest-assistant priest-manager-dancer-people). The military system at Zuni is quite simple and, indeed, may be considered merely as an aspect of the priesthoods. The religious societies and _kivas_ appear to have simple two-term authority structures. The economic system appears to have the same structure. The liaison status of _messenger_ is of the ordinary type. Coordination of a system so complex is necessarily a difficult matter, and the coordination is accomplished at Zuni by a diffuse structure which draws in not only the speaker but also the (ritual?) warrior and perhaps the ceremonial clown-police (koyemshi) as well. Here, as in all of the systems, the exact machinery for relating civil and religious authority statuses to each other and to other authority systems (military, economic, etc.) is far from clear.

Terminology of Slavery

A separate part of the economic-political structure is composed of those statuses defined in terms of ownership of man, that is, in terms of slavery. Slavery of some sort appears to have existed in all the North American Indian cultures here sampled except the Eskimo. It is commonly associated with warfare, and the acquisition of slaves is primarily by capture. Except for the Kwakiutl there is no indication of an explicit status for slave owner, the implication apparently being that the warrior who makes the capture is thereby the owner of the slave. It is understandable that the exigencies of Eskimo life appear to have precluded the taking of captives in warfare, and the Eskimo raids on the neighboring Indian tribes aimed at killing the enemy. (The Eskimo term for "warrior" is also translated "Indian killer.") The Kwakiutl, in the nearest approach in these data to the European concept of kingship, have a special term for the "chief's people."

4. Associational Status

A SPECIAL CASE of social organization which cross-cuts the areas of ascribed and achieved status is that produced by the process of association. Associations may be defined as corporate entities with which individuals identify themselves as members. The corporate fiction under which such entities are treated as pseudoindividuals complicates the analysis of the resulting statuses. Associations, like individuals, occupy a position in the social structure defined by rights and duties and supported by sanctions; as with individuals, moreover, a plurality of associations may occupy a single such position. Thus the number of statuses of an associational order in a given society is likely to be smaller than the number of associations. In order to retain the assumptions involved in our original definition of status, it is convenient to assume that, while associations occupy a social position defined as strictly parallel to status, they are nevertheless not individuals, and the position they occupy is therefore not a status. On the other hand, associations involve status; such statuses as are involved in the authority structure of Zuni fraternities, priesthoods, and kivas, for example, have been discussed as examples of achieved status. A real problem is posed by associational change. Here the differentiation of associational functions may be gradual. Some clans may take on social obligations which differentiate them from others, thus coming to occupy a new social position. Thus, while clan memberships are generally analytically equatable, membership in a clan with special ritual or political functions is analytically distinct from membership in a clan without such functions. In view of the subtlety of this problem and of the data which would be required for its resolution, it has seemed advisable for this study to place the burden of proof on the negative side, and to include as statuses only those positions which clearly fit the definition from which we started.

The excursion into associational structure here represented was an unintended consequence of following out the idea of substantive status with which this study began. Because such an excursion seemed to be central to the rounding out of the idea, we must push on to achieve an analytic and taxonomic view which will enable us to examine the associations of the nine Indian societies in our sample generally and comparatively. The structural principles underlying the process of association may, for this purpose, be reduced to nine:

1. Age grading
2. Sex binding
3. Descent
4. Marriage
5. Residence
6. Ranking
7. Ritualization
8. Economic specialization
9. Political differentiation

We may then use these elements in combination to define the associational typology necessary for describing the Indian societies. A close scrutiny of the types of associations represented in the data may be encompassed in a relatively simple and classical set of terms, the definitions of which follow:

1. Band--residence group
2. Cult--ritual group
3. Order--ranked ritual group
4. Deme--exogamous residential descent group
5. Sib--unilinear exogamous descent group
6. Fraternity--age-graded, sex-bound ritual group
7. Tribe--endogamous residential political descent group
8. Priesthood--age-graded, sex-bound occupationally specialized ritual group
9. Fraternal order--ranked, age-graded, sex-bound ritual group
10. Priestly order--ranked, age-graded, sex-bound occupationally specialized ritual group

Other associational terms needed for comparative purposes will be defined in the text. It is convenient to present the associations as roughly falling into the residential, political, kinship, or religious categories.

33

Residential Association

It should be noted immediately that the <u>household</u> (as a
residential economic unit) does not in the technical sense appear in these societies. The familial unit of residence
seems to be defined almost exclusively in terms of kinship,
and the question of the unrelated individual in residence does
not appear to be formally structured in the Indian cultures.
The principal residential unit which does occur is the <u>band</u>.
This often corresponds to the "village" and is, indeed, ex-
tremely difficult to separate from it in ethnographic usage.
Convincing data on Chipewyan bands are lacking; the units
which are described as such appear to be closer to loose
tribes. It does not appear to have been the American Indian
practice to differentiate a series of concentric residential
loyalties, although "villages" or "bands" or vaguely defined
"local groups" are sometimes described as on different levels of generality. It is likely that such differentiations of
level can only be formalized by giving the band political
functions and thus making a tribe of it, or by adding marriage and descent rules and creating a sib-phratry system.
All of the cultures besides the Chipewyan have some definable band structure: the bands of the Shoshone, the bands
and villages of the Eskimo and Algonkin, and the villages of
the Yokuts, Kwakiutl, Choctaw, and Zuni. The Sioux are a
problem case, since it does not appear to be clear whether
the Siouan "demes" or "tipi divisions" or "villages," as
they are sometimes called, are purely residential at some
level or are consistently exogamous and patrilineal in tendency, as Murdock suggests.

Political Association

All nine of the Indian cultures have some unit of association which can probably be called tribal, although there is
considerable difference from group to group in the formality
and explicitness of such structuring. In an effort to assess
the significance of the band and tribe organizations a systematic attempt was made to estimate the number of bands
and tribes in each society. The estimate was based on a
count of the units listed in Swanton (1945); Kroeber (1939)
was used as a check. The results are presented in the following table. The estimate prorates the number of Alaskan

"villages" for the whole Eskimo area, and is undoubtedly an overestimate.

NUMBER AND AVERAGE MEMBERSHIP OF TRIBES AND BANDS IN NINE INDIAN SOCIETIES

Society	Population	Number of Tribes	Population per Tribe	Number of Bands	Population per Band
Chipewyan	6,430	13	495	(?)	(?)
Eskimo	43,300	117	371	620	70
Shoshone	14,500	(?)	(?)	220	66
Sioux	35,000	18	1944	70	500
Algonkin	39,300	25	1572	108	364
Choctaw	23,000	14	1643	149	154
Kwakiutl	4,500	19	237	20	225
Zuni	2,500	1	2500	1	2500
Yokuts	11,000	40	275	56	198

A final note on political association should be added. Larger political units which might be called alliances or leagues of a more or less temporary nature were developed among the Sioux (the Nakota confederacy comprising virtually the entire language group at one time), the Choctaw (usually fairly local leagues of adjacent villages and tribes), the Algonkin (who created such loose political groupings as the Ottawa, Algonkin, and Ojibwa "nations"), and the Zuni (who joined several of the other Pueblos in an ephemeral alliance against the Spaniards). The league idea was the most extensive political conception of the North American Indians, and the population aggregates represented in these examples are probably fairly typical. An estimate of the maximum size of these units might be, for the Sioux 25,000; for the Choctaw 8,000; for the Algonkin 12,000; and for the Pueblos 15,000. None of these groups attained the degree of permanency and integration reached by the famous League of the Iroquois or the Creek Confederacy, but they are otherwise structurally analogous to these better known cases.

Kinship Association

Four of the Indian societies developed sibs: the Algonkin

35

and Kwakiutl had gentes (patrilineal sibs); the Choctaw and Zuni had clans (matrilineal). The Zuni system was differentiated at two levels, being developed into both clans and phratries. The Siouan patrilineal deme may be considered a borderline case. A rough picture of the demography of these units is presented in the table.

NUMBER AND AVERAGE MEMBERSHIP OF SIBS IN FIVE INDIAN SOCIETIES

Society	No. of Sibs	Membership per Sib
Sioux	70 demes	500 per deme
Algonkin	32 gentes	1228 per gens
Choctaw	15 clans	1533 per clan
Kwakiutl	62 gentes	73 per gens
Zuni	23 clans	109 per clan
	13 phratries	192 per phratry

It is interesting to note that the order of magnitude of these figures is strictly comparable to those for political and residential groups, a fact which suggests the close relation between these units in other than analytic terms. It is also noteworthy that the Eskimo, Chipewyan, Yokuts, and Shoshone exogamous unit (the family within first-cousin relationship) implies a unit of close to the size of the "average" Kwakiutl gens (i.e., somewhat under 70) to which the incest taboo applies. It is worth remembering that the mean membership of these units gives us no hint of the maximum and minimum values of membership.

Religious Association

One or another of the nine societies in our sample has an association in each of the analytic categories we have defined as cult, order, fraternity, priesthood, fraternal order, and priestly order. No one society has all of these, although Zuni comes close. The terminology used to describe and classify such religious associations in the ethnographic reports is peculiarly ambiguous, and it is consequently very difficult to classify some of these associations. Most of them, however, seem to fit more or less easily into our typology.

36

A cult, or purely ritual group, can exist independent of age-grading only where descent or residence can be invoked to guarantee the early and more or less random identification of infants with the group. Consequently, a pure cult group which is simultaneously independent of age, descent, and residence is probably impossible. Residential ritual groups (such as the parish, diocese, etc.) are not found among the Indian groups; ritual descent groups, however, are common. Although the term is not restricted to this usage, "moiety" is perhaps the commonest appellation of such groupings, and the Yokuts ceremonial moiety is a good example, although the descent mechanism for recruiting membership is not clear.

Most of the Indian associations which are loosely called "cult groups" are actually structured by age and sex, and hence fall into the category of groups we have called fraternities. The Shoshone "societies," the Sioux "cults" and "dance societies," the Kwakiutl "divisions" and "dance societies," and the Zuni kivas, "kachina society," and kachina impersonations belong here. The Shoshone have six fraternities, two among the Shoshone of the Basin and four different ones among the Comanche on the Plains. This, it should be noted, is one of the few cases where dialect, region, or subculture appears to make a difference in the status structure. The Sioux have 63 fraternities variously called "age societies," "dance societies," and "cults." If these are differentiated at all, the differentiations appear to be incipient and vague rather than highly structured and specific; therefore, no distinction is made here between the possible subtypes. A minority of the Sioux "fraternities" are women's groups. The Kwakiutl have 54 fraternities closely resembling those of the Sioux in structure. As in the case of the Sioux there is very likely some tendency towards age-grading between associations as well as in differentiating the fraternity members from the general population, and there is also in both cases an incipient ranking system, some associations having higher prestige than others, but again this is unspecific. Several of the Kwakiutl fraternities are subdivided into male and female branches or "divisions," but the structure of these is identical with those fraternities in which the division is indicated by a separate name. The fraternity structure of Zuni is more complex. It appears that virtually all males are initiated into the Kachina Society

37

at six to ten years of age, and it is from this general fraternity that the impersonators of the kachinas seem to be drawn.
At about the same age virtually all males acquire their membership in one of the six kivas, and it appears to be the case
that specific kivas have a responsibility for specific impersonations in at least some cases. Some 163 kachina impersonations are known, and these are represented in the ceremonials in groups and pairs in relation to specific ceremonies. Zuni, therefore, may be said to have three types of
pure fraternities: the Kachina Society, the six kivas and an
unknown number of kachina groups. The ethnographic ac-
counts are somewhat unspecific on its structure, but it is
possible that the Jimsonweed Cult of the Yokuts is a fraternity in structure. In the absence of any specific evidence,
we have omitted it.

Two of the societies appear to have true priesthoods as
technically defined: Algonkin and Zuni. Four of the societies
(Chipewyan, Eskimo, Shoshone, and Yokuts) appear to be
completely devoid of this form of association, and the Sioux
and Kwakiutl have fraternities with names indicating a membership of shamans, but we are not told whether they are exclusively professional. The Choctaw appear to have incor-
porated their priesthoods completely into their system of
military-religious-political "ranks" or orders.

The Algonkin Midewiwin presents a simple case of priesthood: it is age-graded, sex-bound, and restricted to shamans. The Zuni priesthoods are compound, including the
"curing fraternities" together with their component "orders"
and "divisions" as well as the 14 directing "priesthoods" and
the somewhat distinct scalp priesthood. Zuni has 13 curing
priesthoods, members of which also belong to one or another of the 14 cross-cutting subpriesthoods or "orders." Some
of the orders are further subdivided into one or another of
four divisions. The 14 rain priesthoods and scalp priesthood
are differentiated sharply from these curing associations by
their generic functions in connection with the village-wide
ceremonials. Zuni may therefore be said to have 15 general
and 13 curing priesthoods, 14 curing subpriesthoods and
four divisions of the subpriesthoods.

The existence of a pure order, or ranked ritual group,
like the existence of a pure cult, is dependent on the elimi-
nation of age, residence, and descent as factors. Such a
structure is probably theoretically impossible and must cer-

tainly be very rare. Perhaps the nearest approach in our sample are the age-graded orders of the Kwakiutl moiety system. Here in the moiety, memberships are dependent upon membership in one or another of the fraternal orders of the Kwakiutl ceremonial system, and since membership in these fraternal orders begins at about age six, the orders (or "moieties") must be considered age-graded. That they are ranked is indicated in the names (Seals and Commoners), but the consistency with which this criterion is applied is not clear.

Two examples may be cited in these data of fraternal orders (fraternities to which the element of rank has been added): the Choctaw rank system, and the Kwakiutl "ceremonial associations." The position of the Zuni koyemshi is unclear in this connection, since it is difficult to determine whether the West or Koyemshi priesthood is identical with the group of ten masked koyemshi (ceremonial clown-police) who appear at ceremonials, or only shares the name with that group. On the assumption of an identity of the two groups, we may classify the association as a priestly order. The Choctaw rank system is made up of seven levels, and although the exact order of precedence is not clear they appear to be all male and strictly age-graded, and to combine the features of a military rank system with those of a structure of political and religious authority. The Kwakiutl "ceremonial associations" are 20 in number, ten belonging to each of the orders (or ranked "moieties"). Three in each moiety are female, the remaining seven male. All are age-graded as well as sex-bound and strictly ranked, although some of the names suggest the intrusion of other criteria of membership, military ("sick and lame") or political ("head chiefs").

Aside from the ten-rank Koyemshi priesthood already mentioned, the single example in these societies of a priestly order is the Zuni "moiety" system. Although this is implied rather than directly stated in the ethnographies, it appears to be the case that the Night and Day Moieties, to one or the other of which each of the 14 directive priesthoods is assigned, are considered as rank groups and that the priesthoods of the Day Moiety have greater prestige and consequent religious and political authority.

Having completed our survey of the associational structure of the nine Indian societies, we are now in a position to

39

re-examine the question of associational statuses. We may start by tabulating the number of associations. The total number of associations listed for the Chipewyan and Shoshone is undoubtedly an underestimate, but reliable data on the bands of the one and the tribes of the other do not appear to be available.

NUMBER OF ASSOCIATIONS IN NINE INDIAN SOCIETIES BY TYPE

	Chipewyan	Eskimo	Shoshone	Sioux	Algonkin	Choctaw	Kwakiutl	Zuni	Yokuts
Band	(?)	620	220	70	108	149	20	1	56
Tribe	13	117	(?)	18	25	14	19	1	40
League	..	..	..	x	x	x	..	x	..
Sib	..	..	..	70	32	15	62	23	..
								13	
Cult	..	..	..	..	..	..	..	..	2
Order	..	..	..	..	..	..	2	..	..
Fraternity	..	..	6	63	..	..	54	6	..
								1	
Priesthood	..	..	..	..	1	..	2	28	..
								18	
Fraternal order	..	..	..	..	..	7	20	..	..
Priestly order	..	..	..	..	..	..	..	10	..
								2	
Total	13	737	226	221	166	185	179	103	98

Since the authority systems, ritual statuses, and other aspects of the internal structure of associations have been discussed in relation to achieved status, it remains only for us to determine the number of status positions implied by simple membership in these various associations. The actual terms for indicating these relationships are reported but rarely; we are accordingly forced to the expedient of deriving the minimum number of presumptive statuses indicated by the structural differentiations inherent in the associational systems.

For the band these minimum statuses would appear to be

"own band member" and "other band member." For the tribe
we may assume "tribesman," "member of a friendly tribe,"
and "enemy." Where the league or alliance appears, we may
probably add "ally." In the case of sibs, the minimum statuses would be "mother's clansman," "father's clansman,"
"member of a linked clan" (i.e., within the same phratry),
and "member of strange clan." For the cult we may assume
"member of own cult" and "member of other cult." The fraternities and priesthoods, being age-graded and sex-bound,
do not imply (although they do not preclude) the ego reference of the foregoing associations, but we may assume
"member" as a minimal status in each case. The orders,
fraternal orders, and priestly orders, involving as they do
the principle of rank, are necessarily status-differentiated
at least in proportion to the number of ranks recognized,
since each rank must by definition involve distinct rights
and duties for its occupant.

The terms actually found for these relationships may be
reported briefly: tribesman (Kwakiutl t'ensila; Yokuts
yokochnim, "my people"); friend (Algonkin djiwan; Choctaw
inkana; Kwakiutl qasta; Zuni kihe, "ceremonial friend");
enemy (Chipewyan enda; Shoshone taivo, "alien"; Algonkin
nodawe; Choctaw tanap; Zuni abachu; Yokuts lagl'in'in, "for-
eigner"); ally (Sioux nakota; Choctaw apepoa); clansman
(Choctaw imokla); stranger (Choctaw imongolasha, "member of opposite clan"); cult mate (Yokuts noche, "moiety
member"); member (Zuni tikyili). The terminology for the
Choctaw and Kwakiutl rank systems is presented in the following tables.

CHOCTAW FRATERNAL ORDERS (Male)

1. Hopaii (War Prophets)
2. Holitopa (Holy Men)
3. Holahta (War)
4. Humma (Red)
5. Imastabi (Killer)
6. Hacho (Creek)
7. Imataha (Novices)

KWAKIUTL FRATERNAL ORDERS (Male)

Seals Moiety	Commoners Moiety
1. Hemelk (Head Chiefs)	Moomguana'le (Head Chiefs)
2. Qoqosqimo (Elders)	Ł'eł'exen (Elders)
3. Qoeqoim (Chiefs)	Nentsae (Chiefs)

41

4. Ⱡ'eⱡ'exen (Elders) Ga'gimola (Elders)
5. D'od'opa (Young Men) K'ik'ineⱡa (Sick and lame)
6. Maamx'enox (Youths) Ⱡaalko (Youths)
7. Naanexsoku (Boys) Xixitpa (Boys)

The Kwakiutl have an additional set of three-level women's sororal orders in each moiety, but since they appear to parallel the men's orders closely they require no special treatment.

We may now summarize the number of associational statuses in the nine Indian societies in tabular form.

NUMBER AND TYPE OF ASSOCIATIONAL STATUSES IN NINE INDIAN SOCIETIES

	Chipewyan	Eskimo	Shoshone	Sioux	Algonkin	Choctaw	Kwakiutl	Zuni	Yokuts
Band	2	2	2	2	2	2	2	2	2
Tribe	3	3	3	3	3	3	3	3	3
League	..	..	..	1	1	1	..	1	..
Sib	..	..	..	3	3	3	3	4	..
Cult	..	..	..	..	..	..	..	..	2
Order	..	..	..	..	..	..	2	..	..
Fraternity	..	..	1	1	..	..	1	3	..
Fraternal order	..	..	..	..	..	7	7	..	..
Priestly order	..	..	..	..	..	..	..	12	..
Priesthood	..	..	..	..	1	..	..	4	..
Total	5	5	6	10	10	16	18	29	7
Miscellaneous	..	3	..	2	1	1	..	2	1
Total	5	8	6	12	11	17	18	31	8

It is noteworthy in relation to associational structure that none of these American Indian societies possess associations of an economic type, or, with the exception of the tribe and the rather dubious case of the Zuni "council," of the political type. Certain informal or relatively informal arrangements in some of these societies would seem to indicate that this aspect of social structure was undeveloped rather than totally lacking. Such terms as the Eskimo tuvark (hunting companion), and the Yokuts kapas (partner), and the Choctaw apelachi (partner) may perhaps be indicative of a rudimentary form of economic association. More or less related to these in part are the terms of ceremonial kinship: Sioux hunka (adopted relative) or ateya (foster father), Eskimo saunirk (namesake) or arnakata (wife-exchange partner), Algonkin awan a (namesake) or the Zuni ceremonial father and son. These terms have been added to the above table as "miscellaneous" statuses.

In the interest of analytic completeness, one final set of statuses may be added, namely, the special term used by each of these cultural groups for itself. These are: dene (Chipewyan), inuk (Eskimo), numu (Shoshone), nakota (Sioux), djibwe (Algonkin), chahta (Choctaw), kwaguł (Kwakiutl), ashiwi (Zuni), and yokuts (Yokuts). These terms are not included in the tabulations and computations which follow.

5. Cultural Complexity and Social Structure

IN ORDER TO TEST the theoretical significance of the approach to status outlined here, we may set up a number of hypotheses about the number of status terms in a given society. We have aimed these hypotheses at an exploration of the relation between the number of status terms and cultural complexity. We may perhaps begin with a summary table showing the number of status terms discovered for each of the nine cultures.

The subtotals in the table (facing page) have considerable bearing on the statistical argument which follows, and should be made clear. The subtotal of ascribed statuses represents the figure for that area of social structure with duplications due to the existence of alternative systems eliminated. In the achieved status structure, substatuses have been similarly eliminated. For completeness' sake, the statistical tests of significance were computed on both subtotals and totals in each case.

It was initially hypothesized that the common assumption of a relationship between gross population size and cultural complexity should apply to the societies in our sample. This may be framed as a general hypothesis:

1. There should be a positive correlation between total number of status terms and gross population size.

The closer examination of the data made this hypothesis seem more and more crude and less and less likely. The statistical test of the hypothesis was nonetheless made, and the correlation was found not to differ significantly from zero at the .05 per cent level of significance. The hypothesis was accordingly rejected.

NUMBER AND TYPE OF STATUS TERMS
IN NINE INDIAN CULTURES

	Chipewyan	Eskimo	Shoshone	Sioux	Algonkin	Choctaw	Kwakiutl	Zuni	Yokuts
Ascribed									
Age-Sex	9	9	17	14	11	18	11	11	14
Nuclear	11	14	12	12	12	14	9	13	10
Lineal	2	3	6	9	3	5	10	5	2
Collateral	6	12	6	14	9	8	5	7	8
Affinal	1	..	21	12	8	13	6	2	14
Accidental	3	..	9	9	4	11	9	9	8
Other	..	..	4	2	6	13	3	..	6
Subtotal	32	38	75	72	53	82	53	47	62
Alternative	..	..	4	12	6	..	2	3	6
Total	32	38	79	84	59	82	55	50	68
Achieved									
Magical	2	2	2	1	4	5	5	3	4
Oracular	2	..	2	..	2	..	2	1	3
Fetishistic	..	..	..	1	..	..	1	1	..
Technology	2	2	4	2	5	5	6	7	4
Property	..	2	..	..	..	4	5	5	2
Force	1	1	3	3	3	2	2	1	1
Authority	3	5	9	13	9	10	12	17	7
Slavery	1	..	1	1	1	1	3	1	1
Subtotal	11	12	21	21	24	27	36	36	22
Substatuses	2	9	15	3	4	10	22	9	11
Total	13	21	36	24	28	37	58	45	33
Associational	5	8	6	12	11	17	18	31	8
Grand Total	50	67	121	120	98	136	131	126	109

In refining the indices of cultural complexity and the analysis of status terminologies, we have differentiated ascribed,
achieved, and associational status. The analysis of associa-

tional status has carried us through an analysis of associations as such, and thus makes available another potential measure of complexity: gross number of associations. Estimates of population density have also been drawn up, based upon Kroeber's estimates (1939), but corrected for the fact that the cultural units have here been linguistically defined. As a measure of complexity drawn from a somewhat different range of data, Kroeber's index of "cultural intensity" was abstracted from the same source (Kroeber, 1939:131-41). The data on population size and density and "cultural intensity" are presented in the following table.

POPULATION DENSITY AND INTENSITY
IN NINE INDIAN CULTURES

Culture	Population	Area Square Kilometers	Density Pop. /1 sq. Kilometer	Intensity
Chipewyan	6,430	14,330	0.45	1
Eskimo	43,300	19,046	2.27	2
Shoshone	14,500	4,462	3.25	1
Sioux	35,000	6,410	5.46	3+
Algonkin	39,300	5,658	6.95	2
Choctaw	23,000	1,549	14.85	4+
Kwakiutl	4,500	211	21.30	4+
Zuni	2,500	114	21.90	5+
Yokuts	11,000	382	28.79	3-

To test the hypothesis of no significant differences between cultures in number of ascribed, achieved, and associational statuses and number of associations, a rank-order analysis of variance (Moses, 1952:130-32) was performed on the subtotals in the table on page 45 together with the gross number of associations listed in the table on page 40. The Chi-square value obtained of 36.65, significant at better than the 0.01 level, indicated that the differences between the ranks of the various cultures in number of ascribed, achieved, and associational statuses and gross number of associations are not due to chance.

In the discussion of ascribed status above, it was argued that there was very likely an upper limit to the number of possible ascribed statuses, and that this number was likely to be approached even in very simple cultures. On this assumption, we may frame the hypothesis that:

2. There should be no correlation between the number of ascribed status terms and cultural intensity, population size, or population density.

Since achieved status terms are under no such structural limitation, it seems reasonable to suppose that they will tend to multiply as the culture grows more complex. On the assumption that such progressive complexity is related to population density and cultural intensity but not necessarily to population size, we may frame the hypothesis that:

3. There should be a positive correlation between the number of achieved status terms and cultural intensity or population density, but no correlation between that number and population size.

Because associations may be formed very flexibly by the process of naming groups and giving them duties to perform, and because this process would appear to be less strictly dependent on technological or scientific knowledge than is the case for considerable areas of general achieved status structure, it seems reasonable to assume that associational status will bear an even closer relationship to the increasing complexity of cultural systems than will general achieved status. Accordingly, we may hypothesize that:

4. There should be a high positive correlation between the number of associational status terms and cultural intensity or population density, but no correlation between that number and population size.

Because sheer numbers in a small and relatively simple association may become unwieldy, leading to the multiplication of associations by imitative reduplication requiring a very low level of cultural "invention" or learning, we might expect that the gross number of associations would be related to population size but not to cultural complexity. Accordingly:

5. There should be a positive correlation between the number of associations and population size, but no correlation between that number and population density or cultural intensity.

The wide margin for error in all of the data makes any elaborate statistical procedures difficult. The hypotheses have been tested using a rank-order correlation coefficient. The results are presented in the following table. The standard error of the rank-order correlation coefficient is an approximate probability measure only, based on a constant correction factor rather than on actual computations from the variability of the data. The standard error becomes particularly unreliable as the correlation approaches unity. It should also be noted that the error involved in the use of this measure decreases as the sample size increases. The present sample is, from this viewpoint, relatively small.

RANK CORRELATION COEFFICIENTS BETWEEN MEASURES OF CULTURAL COMPLEXITY AND STATUS

	Density	Intensity	Population
Ascribed Status Subtotal	+0.30 (±0.32)	+0.21 (±0.33)	+0.19 (±0.34)
Ascribed Status Total	+0.27 (±0.32)	+0.22 (±0.34)	+0.28 (±0.32)
Achieved Status Subtotal	+0.82 (±0.11)*	+0.83 (±0.11)*	+0.45 (±0.28)
Achieved Status Total	+0.73 (±0.16)*	+0.70 (±0.18)*	+0.55 (±0.24)†
Associational Status	+0.66 (±0.20)*	+0.95 (±0.33)*	+0.33 (±0.31)
Number of Associations	-0.35 (±0.31)	-0.06 (±0.34)	-0.62 (±0.31)†
Total Statuses	+0.58 (±0.31)	+0.74 (±0.16)*	+0.37 (±0.30)

* z-score probability less than .01.
† z-score probability less than .05, but more than .01.

The correlations were converted to z-scores in order to test the hypothesis that each correlation did not differ significantly from zero. As may be seen from the probability levels indicated in the table, the hypothesis that the correlations do not differ from zero may be rejected at better than the .01 per cent level for the correlations between population density and achieved and associational status, between cultural intensity and the same factors, and between cultural intensity and the total number of statuses. The same hypothesis may be rejected at better than the .05 per cent level for the correlation between population size and total number of achieved statuses and between population size and number of associations. All of the correlations which thus appear to be significant are positive except the last.

The significant departures from zero of some of the correlations make possible a test of the hypotheses we have stated. Hypothesis 2 stated the expectation of no correlation between the number of ascribed-status terms and the measures of cultural intensity, population size, or population density. This accords with the empirical correlations, which do not differ significantly from zero, either in the "subtotal" or "total" computations.

Hypothesis 3 stated the expectation of a positive correlation between the number of achieved-status terms and cultural intensity or population density but no correlation with population size. Two sets of correlations are relevant to this hypothesis, since we have tested it against the "subtotal" of achieved-status terms (from which the substatuses were eliminated) and against the "total" of those terms (including substatuses). In both cases significant positive correlations were obtained between the number of achieved-status terms and the measures of population density and intensity. The correlation between number of achieved-status terms and population size does not differ significantly from zero on the "subtotal" correlation. Thus far the hypothetical expectation is upheld. On the "total" achieved-status data, however, a positive correlation of 0.55 ($\pm$0.24) differs from zero at the .05 per cent level of confidence, although it is not significant at the .01 per cent level. It is possible that the substatus differentiation represented in these data is in fact partially correlated with gross population size.

Hypothesis 4 set up the expectation of a high positive correlation between the number of associational-status terms and cultural intensity or population density, but no correlation with population size. The empirical correlations correspond to this expectation, except that the implication that these correlations should be higher than those between measures of cultural complexity and achieved status is not borne out by the evidence. A larger sample might give us the discriminative power to test this implication statistically.

Hypothesis 5 stated our expectation of a positive correlation between the number of associations and population size, but no correlation between number of associations and cultural intensity or population density. The empirical correla-

49

tions between number of associations and cultural intensity and between number of associations and population density do not deviate significantly from zero. On the basis of these data we must reject, however, the hypothesis of positive correlation between number of associations and population size; the empirical correlation, differing significantly from zero at the .05 per cent level, was <u>negative</u>: -0.62 (± 0.31). It is likely in this connection that our data are not altogether typical, since it happens that our most "complex" cultures (Kwakiutl and Zuni) happen to have the smallest populations. It is unlikely that a larger sample would continue to display this negative relationship between population size and cultural complexity, and consequently unlikely that the negative correlation here obtained would hold in a larger sample.

Because our argument has been couched in terms of differentiable types of status terms, no general relationship was thought to be theoretically arguable between the total number of status terms and measures of cultural complexity, at least for the range of these very small and relatively simple societies. It seemed useful for completeness, however, to formulate a purely statistical hypothesis on this relationship, even though the confounding of theoretical variables makes any inference difficult. Hypothesis 6 was framed, therefore, on the arbitrary assumption that there should be no correlation between total number of status terms and population density or cultural intensity. Empirical correlations were accordingly run, and although the correlation of population density and total number of statuses did not differ from zero at the .05 per cent level of significance, a high correlation of $+0.74$ (± 0.16), significantly different from zero at the .01 per cent level, was found to obtain between total number of status terms and Kroeber's index of cultural intensity. This unexpected finding is difficult to interpret in the absence of a related correlation with population density, elsewhere in this sample associated with intensity. It is possible, of course, that Kroeber's judgments of cultural intensity were weighted towards general cultural factors which correlate more highly with the summative total number of status terms than with the more stringently defined structural categories used in our hypotheses.

6. Conclusion

THE PRESENT STUDY is an essay in method: the method of status terminology. We have already discussed some of the advantages of the method. It furnishes us with a means of being "objectively subjective" in the study of social structure. It provides a broad and yet precise basis for cross-cultural comparisons without prejudging the categories in terms of which such comparisons will be made. It represents only an amplification and explicit development of what ethnographers are already doing, and hence does not violate the continuity of development of method in the field. It does not require any elaborate training or special skills beyond those normally expected of the field-working anthropologist. It is consistent with a variety of theoretical and empirical interests. It places the study of the entire social structure of a given culture on a theoretically consistent basis, thus making possible an explicit and potentially exhaustive "map" of a society, and in so doing it points up gaps in descriptions and analyses of particular societies.

In order to explore the limitations, as well as the advantages, of the terminological approach to status, we have applied it to two problems. The first problem, comprising the body of this study, was to create an analytic taxonomy of status to serve as a framework for description and comparison of different social systems. In order to ensure a workable simplicity in the systems, nine American Indian societies were selected: Eskimo, Chipewyan, Shoshone, Kwakiutl, Yokuts, Zuni, Sioux, Algonkin, and Choctaw. The status terminologies of these societies were then presented and analyzed in detail. Broadly, we found it necessary to divide our analysis into three areas, namely, those of as-cribed, achieved, and associational status. The ascribed-status systems were then described in terms of the structural factors of age, sex, mating, generation, and death, and the differences between systems were pointed up with respect to generalization, alternatives, and reciprocity. The achieved statuses were analyzed in terms of religious, economic, and political structure, each subdivided in terms of power, communication, and ownership. Associational status was analyzed in terms of the structural factors of age, sex, descent, marriage, residence, ranking, ritualization, economic specialization, and politics. The types of associations actually occurring in the data were bands, tribes, cults, orders, demes, sibs, fraternities, priesthoods, fraternal orders, priestly orders, and leagues. From a consideration of associational structure we were led gradually to the conception of memberships as distinct from statuses. Thus the six kivas at Zuni imply six types of membership, but each kiva is structurally identical with each other one (they are all fraternities, or age-graded, sex-bound ritual groups), and there is, therefore, only one kind of status implied.

In more general terms, the study of the associational structure of these nine Indian groups led us to reformulate somewhat our initial conceptions. Associations, like individuals, occupy positions in society defined in terms of rights and duties. By our original definition such positions are not statuses, although they closely resemble them, just as associations are not individuals although they may be (as in the United States) legally classified as such. Associational position is thus, like status, a special form of social position, but when positions are occupied by individuals we have preserved our usage and called them statuses; where they are occupied by corporate entities (or "pseudoindividuals") the term associational position seems more precise.

The second problem on which we have tested the terminological method lies in the theoretical area of cultural complexity. From theoretical consideration of this area five hypotheses were derived and tested. The expectation of a general positive correlation between number of status terms and population size was not upheld in our data, although it is likely that a broader sample might reverse this finding. Positive correlations between the number of achieved- and associational-status terms and population density and cultural intensity were hypothesized and demonstrated. Population size was shown to be unrelated to these measures. The number of ascribed-status terms was shown to be uncorrelated with population size or density or cultural intensity, as had been hypothesized. The number of associations proved to be uncorrelated with cultural intensity and population density as expected but revealed a significant negative correlation between number of associations and population size where the hypothetical expectation was a positive correlation. Finally, a positive correlation appeared between cultural intensity and total number of status terms where no correlation had been hypothesized.

Our theoretical assumptions were that cultural complexity should be developmentally definable as closely associated with division of labor (of which we might consider population density a crude measure) on the one hand and with cultural elaboration (of which Kroeber's index of cultural intensity appears to be a rating) on the other.

These assumptions appear to accord well with our empirical findings. The fundamentally linguistic definition of our cultural units in the first place seemed to make gross population size an irrelevant variable, at least for the range of societies we were considering. The number of associations was presumed to have some relationship to this on the assumption that at least certain types of associations (bands, for example) would tend to multiply reduplicatively rather than to grow in size as the culture expanded in population, it being assumed that there is no increase in cultural complexity. These assumptions do not work out so satisfactorily in the evidence, which may indicate a confounding of variables in the association enumeration, or may be attributable to sampling inadequacies. In general we may conclude that what is commonly called cultural complexity is closely related to the number of achieved and associational statuses in a society.

Two examples of the application of the terminological method to status have been examined closely in this paper. Other fields of application are open in a variety of directions. One such field which would appear to be ripe for this method of research is the field of what might be called "social demography." Kroeber's pioneer study of the social demography of the Zuni (1917), tracing the incidence of Zuni clan status throughout the social system, gives us a precise, even quantitative, knowledge of Zuni society which can scarcely be matched in North American ethnology. Warner and Lunt's volume on the status systems of Yankee City (1942) explores the same field with relation to class. An explicitly terminological approach to status opens up the path suggested by these studies for a complete census of the distribution of individuals in a social system, exhaustively described. It places on a firm empirical basis the question of the coincidence of statuses in each particular system.

Beyond the mere statement of the existence of specific statuses and the analysis of their interrelations, and beyond the study of the distribution of individuals in these categories provided by the social system, we may also use status terminology as a springboard to problems in social dynamics. We have here been concerned primarily with status and with social statics; role problems have accordingly been left unstated and the role implications of the data ignored. If we cling to the commonly accepted dictum that there is no role without status and no status without role, it must be noted that there are certain inconsistencies in usage between the concept status as here defined and some usages of the concept role. Terms descriptive of role are rather commonly applied from the viewpoint of the scientific observer; thus we speak of a "passive role" or a "deviant role." Such usages do not appear to have status counterparts. This and other inconsistencies have to be clarified before status and role can become the twin concepts which many theorists would have them be.

Assuming these problems to be capable of resolution, the terminological method can be of considerable utility for social dynamics. The concepts of socialization, stereotyping, attitude formation, status personality, and life career line may be efficiently approached from this angle. If status terms can enable us to systematize our knowledge of these phenomena on a comparative basis, they may well aid in closing the gap presently existing between structural and dynamic research.

Our concern in the body of this study has been with the implications of status terminology as a technique and as a method. A final word should be added on the theoretical implications of this approach, to make explicit the theoretical connections which are explored in detail throughout the study. Although our starting point was the concept of status and our field that of social organization, we have been compelled to follow the ramifications of our method all over the theoretical map. Such concepts as culture, society, association, and system have perforce crept in; distinctions of ascribed and achieved status, of positions and memberships, of functional and historical diversification have had to be recognized; cultural complexity and a particular view of its nature have been treated; questions of methodology and of inference, of definition and conclusion, of pattern and taxonomy have obtruded themselves at many points. A good method should probably be independent, at least to a degree, of opinions on many of these topics, however professional. It is hoped that this method will prove to be so. The theoretical setting in which it is here placed has been "functionalist" in its search for analytic universals, "structural" in its emphasis on the uniqueness of analytic elements, "historical" in its preservation of the configurational uniqueness of each cultural system, "empiricist" in its insistence on clear operational significance of the major variables. The theory has, in short, been eclectic; if, however, this exploration of the concept status should aid in the construction of a more adequate methodology and theory drawing on these or other currents of professional thought, its aim will have been served.

Appendix

In the listing of status terms, the native terms are given whenever possible. Substatuses are differentiated from primary statuses by indention (see p. 18). In order to clarify the status systems in the various dimensions of analysis, some terms are listed more than once, but they are numbered only in the context to which they are primarily relevant.

AGE-SEX

Chipewyan

1. dezona (baby)
2. ekea (boy)
3.   (girl)
4. chileku (young man)
5.   (young woman)
6. deneli (man)
7.   (woman)
8.   (old man)
9.   (old woman)

Eskimo

1.   (baby?)
2.   (boy?)
3.   (girl?)
4.   (young man?)
5.   (young woman?)
6. inuk (man)
7. arnaq (woman)
8.   (old man?)
9.   (old woman?)

Shoshone

1. duhai'aii (infant)
2. oma'a (baby)
3. natsi'i (baby boy)
4. watsua'a (baby girl)
5. nomadagi (adolescent)

Sioux

1. hoksishala (baby)
2. wakan-heza (child)
3. hoksi (boy)
4. wi-shinsha (girl)
5. wisho-koska (young person)

56

6. tupitsii (boy)
7. tsuadum (girl)
8. budunyawa (youth)
9. nana yukwi'i (young man)
10. mogwo'um (young woman)
11.   (adult)
12. nana (man)
13. piawabi (woman)
14. muatupu (old person)
15. wa'itsi (old man)
16. hubuchi'i (old woman)
17. dubas (berdache)

6. koska (young man)
7. wi-koska (young woman)
8. wisho-tanka (adult)
9. wisha-sa (man)
10. wino-hinsha (woman)
11. wisho-kan (old person)
12. wisha-hsha (old man)
13. wino-hsha (old woman)
14. winktan (berdache)

Algonkin

1.   (infant)
2.   (baby)
3. bi (little boy)
4.   (little girl)
5. oshkabewis (young man)
6.   (young woman)
7. nabe (man)
8. noje (woman)
9. kichi'nab (old man)
10.   (old woman)
11.   (berdache)

Choctaw

1. atta ammona (infant)
2. allonsi (suckling infant)
3. puskus (baby)
4. alla (child)
5. alla nakni (boy)
6. alla tek (girl)
7. himmita (young person)
8. hatak himmita (young man)
9. ohoyo himmita (young woman)
10. asano (adult)
11. hatak (man)
12. ohoyo (woman)
13. pishankichi (elder)
14. hatak sipokni (older man)
15. ohoyo sipokni (older woman)
16. asahnoyechi (aged)
17. hatak kamassallika (old man)
18. kasheho (old woman)

Kwakiutl

1. mayołam (infant)
2.   (baby)
3. ginanama (child)
4. babagam (boy)

Zuni

1.   (infant)
2. cha'le (child)
3.   (boy)
4. ewashtokii (girl)

5.	(girl)	5.	(young man)
6.	(young man)	6.	(young woman)
7.	(young woman)	7.	(man)
8. bagwanem (man)		8.	(woman)
9. ts'edaq (woman)		9. ʎashiḳi (old man)
10. q'ulyaḳu (old man)		10.	(old woman)
11. ʎak'wane (old woman)		11.	(berdache)

Yokuts

1. aktach (infant)
2. witeb (baby)
3. boch'on (boy)
4.　　　(girl)
5.　　　(youth)
6. noch'o (young man)
7. gai'ich' (young woman)
8. bohut'hat' (adult)
9. nocha (man)
10. mukis (woman)
11. modo'o (old person)
12.　　　(old man)
13.　　　(old woman)
14. tonochim (berdache)

NUCLEAR KINSHIP

Chipewyan

1. sete (fa)
2. ene (mo)
3. sechua (so)
4. setua (da)
5. sedone (hu)
6. sezake (wi)
7. sondie (obr)
8. sade (osi)
9. seche (ybr)
10. sete (ysi)
11.　　　(co-wife)

Eskimo

1. ataataq (fa)
2. anaanaq (mo)
3. erneq (so)
4. panik (da)
5. meraq (ch)
6. uve (hu)
7. nuliaq (wi)
8. anik (woobr)
9. aleqa (maosi)
10. nukaq (woybr)
11. nayaq (maysi)
12. angayo (osibsamesex?)
13.　　　(ysibsamesex?)
14. qatangt (sib)

Shoshone

1. 'apu (fa)
2. bia' (mo)
3. dua (so)
4. baidu (da)
5. kumapi (hu)
6. kwi'p (wi)
7. bavi (obr)
8. oadzi (osi)
9. dami (ybr)
10. nami (ysi)
11. samupi (siboppsex)
12. taka (sib)

Sioux

1. atku (fa)
2. hunku (mo)
3. chinkshi (so)
4. chunkshi (da)
5. wishilo (favorite so)
6. chaske (firstborn so)
7. wi-tokape (firstborn da)
8. hepan (secondborn so)
9. hapan (secondborn da)
10. hepi (thirdborn so)
11. hepistanna (thirdborn da)
12. chatan (fourthborn so)
13. wanska (fourthborn da)
14. hake (fifthborn so)
15. wi-hake (fifthborn da)
16. hakata (lastborn ch)
17. kichiminga (sp)
18. hinkna (hu)
19. tawin (wi)
20. bluze (polygynous hu)
21. tayak (nonsororal pl. wi)
22. mitayak (sororal pl. wi)
23. winu (captured wi)
24. tawichu (wi of consummat-
    ed marriage)
25. chive (maobr)
26. timnona (woobr)
27. tanke (maosi)
28. chunwe (woosi)
29. sunka (ybr)
30. tankasi (maysi)
31. tanka (woysi)

Algonkin

1. nos (fa)
2. niinga (mo)
3. nichanis (ch)
4. gwizis (so)
5. danis (da)
6. wiiwa (hu)

Choctaw

1. inki (fa)
2. ishki (mo)
3. iso (ch)
4. nakni (so)
5. tek (da)
6. allahpi (firstborn so)

59

7. naabem (wi)
8. wikimaagan (sp)
9. kush (co-wi)
10. sayen (obr)
11. misen (osi)
12. shimen (ysib)
13. chkiwazi (mabr)
14. chi'kwe (wosi)
15. dawena (siboppsex)

7. inkiichapa (older so)
8. alla isht aiopi (youngest ch)
9. inhatak (hu)
10. itekchi (wi)
11. itunchukali (sp)
12. imanni (osibsamesex)
13. inakfish (siboppsex)
14. intek (siboppsex)
15. itichapa (oldest brother)

Kwakiutl

1. adats (fa)
2. abamp (mo)
3. gigaoⱡnuku (pa)
4. xonoku (so)
5. xonokwas (da)
6. ⱡaewunam (hu)
7. qenem (wi)
8. enola (osib)
9. ts'aewe (ysib?)
10. enamoku (sibsamesex)
11. waq'wa (siboppsex)

Zuni

1. tatchu (fa)
2. tsitta (mo)
3. cha'le (ch)
4. aktsekyi (so)
5. k'yatsekyi (da)
6. oyyemshi (hu)
7. oyye (wi)
8. pappa (obr)
9. kyawwu (osi)
10. suwe (maybr)
11. ikyinna (maysi)
12. hanni (woysib)
13. hashi (maosi)

Yokuts

1. natet (fa)
2. nasos (mo)
3.   (so)
4. 'axil (da)
5. polum (hu)
6. mokiy (wi)
7. nibech' (obr)
8. na'at (osi)
9. ne'es (ybr)
10. no'od (ysi)

LINEAL KINSHIP

Chipewyan

1. sezia (grfa)
2. setsun (grmo)
   (grso-ybr)
   (grda-da)

Shoshone

1. kunu' (fafa-masoch)
2. hutsi (famo-wosoch)
3. toko' (mofa-madach)
4. kaku' (momo-wodach)
5. dza'a (grgrpa-grgrch)
6. kucho (grgrgrpa-grgrgrch)

Algonkin

1. mishomis (grfa)
2. nokomis (grmo)
3. nochis (grch)

Kwakiutl

1. ewats (grfa)
2. ewadzaga (grmo)
3. ts'oxułama (grso)
4. ts'oxułamagas (grda)
5. helo (grgrpa)
6. helokwine (grgrso)
7. helokwinegas (grgrda)
8. edatae (grgrch)
9. qwesalis gagamp (grgrgr-fa)
10. qwesanxalis gagamp (grgr-grgrfa)

Eskimo

1.   (grfa)
2.   (grmo)
3.   (grch)

Sioux

1. tunkan (grfa)
2. tunkansi (mofa)
3. tunkansila (fafa)
4.   (grmo?)
5. kun(si) (famo)
6. onshi(si) (momo)
7. tokaza (grch)
8. wicha-tokaza (grso)
9. wino-tokaza (grda)

Choctaw

1. imafo (grfa)
2. ipokni (grmo)
3. ipok (grch)
4. ipok nakni (grso)
5. ipok tek (grda)

Zuni

1. nana (grfa-grso)
2. wowwo (famo-wosoda)
3. hotta (momo-wodada)
4.   (grmo-grda?)
5. toshle (grso)
6. alle (grgrso)
7. awan-nana (grgrfa-grgrch)
8. uwaikiami (grgrso)

Yokuts

1. 'enas (grfa-grso)
2. kamich' (grmo-grda?)
3. duda (momo-wodach)
4. bap'e (famo-wosoch)

COLLATERAL KINSHIP

Chipewyan

1. seta (fabr)
2. sanbe (fasi)
3. saze (mobr)
4. son (mosi)
5. aya (wobrch)
6. sayaze (wosich)
       (masibso-so)
       (masibda-da)

Eskimo

1. akak (fabr)
2. atsaq (fasi)
3. angak (mobr)
4. aya (mosi)
5.   (mabrch)
6.   (wobrch)
7.   (masich)
8.   (wosich)
9.   (omaleco)
10.   (ymaleco)
11.   (ofemaleco)
12.   (yfemaleco)

Shoshone

1. hai' (fabr-mabrch)
2. baha (fasi-wobrch)
3. 'ara' (mobr-masich)
4. biatsi (mosi-wosich)
5. haish (male co)
6. ti'i (female co)
7. bua'a (co)
8. taga (mamaleco)
9. tii (wofemaleco)
10. niwa (cooppsex?)

Sioux

1. nungazin (fabr)
2. tonwin (fasi)
3. nekshi (mobr)
4. shanin (mosi)
     (mabrso-so?)
5. tozan (wobrso)
6. tahansi (masiso)
7. tonsk (masioso)
8. tonska (masiyso)
9. tonzan (mabrda?)
10. toska (wobrda)
11. hankasi (masida)
      (wosich-ch?)
12. hunkasi (parallel co)
      (mafasiso-fa?)
      (mafasida-fasi?)
13. sichesi (wofasiso)

Sioux

14. <u>sichepansi</u> (wofasida)
(mamobrso-so?)
(mamobrda-mabr-
da?)
(womobrso-so?)
(womobrda-wobr-
da?)

Algonkin

Choctaw

1. <u>mishome</u> (fabr)
2. <u>ze'gas</u> (fasi)
3. <u>jishe</u> (mobr)
4. <u>no'sha</u> (mosi)
5. <u>do'jim</u> (mabrso)
6. <u>do'jimi</u> kwem (mabrda)
7. <u>do'jimis</u> (wosich)
8. <u>ningwanis</u> (siboppsexso)
9. <u>shimis</u> (siboppsexda)
10. <u>tawis</u> (malecrossco)
11. <u>dangusha</u> (femalecrossco)
12. <u>nimo'shen</u> (crosscooppsex)

1. <u>inkusi</u> (fabr)
2. <u>inhukni</u> (fasi)
3. <u>immoshi</u> (mobr)
4. <u>ishkusi</u> (mosi)
(brso-so?)
(brda-da?)
5. <u>imbaivi</u> (siso)
6. <u>imbitek</u> (sida)
(parallel cosib)
(fasiso-fa)
(fasida-fasi)
7. (mobrso?)
8. (mobrda?)

Kwakiutl

Zuni

1. <u>q'ule</u> (uncle)
2. <u>anes</u> (aunt)
3. <u>ʸoele</u> (nephew)
4. <u>ʸoelega</u> (niece)
(co-sib)
5. <u>q'ulek'ot</u> (paco)

1. <u>tatchu tsana</u> (fabr)
2. <u>kukku</u> (fasi)
3. <u>kyakkya</u> (mobr)
4. <u>tsitta tsana</u> (mosi)
(mabrch-ch)
5. <u>talle</u> (wobrso)
6. <u>eyye</u> (sich)
7. <u>kyasse</u> (sich)
(parallel co-sib)
(fasiso-fa)
(fasida-fasi)
(womobrso-wobrso)
(womobrda-wobrda)
(mamobrso-so)
(mamobrda-da)

Yokuts

1. kom'ovis (fabr)
2. nusos (fasi)
3. 'agas (mobr)
4. niked (mosi)
5. 'aw'hay' (sibch)
6.   (sibso?)
7. gats'ap (sibda)
8.   (mabrch?)
9.   (wobrch?)
10. ts'ayax (masich)
11.   (wosich?)
12.   (co-sib)

AFFINAL KINSHIP

Chipewyan

(spfa-grfa)
(spmo-grmo)
(dahu-ybr)
(sowi-da)
1. saye (sib-inlaw)
(avuncular?)
(nepotic)

Eskimo

Shoshone

1. 'arapuitsi (spfa)
2. bahatsi (spmo)
3. nimikuni (hufa)
4. nimihutsi (humo)
5. nimitoko' (wifa)
6. nimikaku' (wimo)
7. dukunu' (dahu)
8. hushipia (sowi)
9. haipia (sib-inlawoppsex)
10. te'tsi (masihu-wibr)
11. bahabiapu (wobrwi-husi)
12. haints (wisi)
13. yage kahni (decwisi)
14. tsi (hubrwi)

Sioux

1. tung (spfa)
2.   (mo-spmo)
3. takos (ch-chsp)
4. omaheton (dahupa)
5. amawaheton (sowipa)
6. tahan (masihu-wibr)
7. sichepan (wobrwi-husi)
8. hanke (wiosi)
9. hanka (wiysi)
10.   (mabrwi?)
11.   (hubr?)
12. siche (wosihu)

Shoshone

15. (wisihu)
16. piavia (faobrwi)
17. tuipia (faybrwi)
18. nagahaipia (fabrwi)
    (avuncular?)
19. nimitso (grpa-inlaw)
20. tso'a'apu (grso-inlaw)
21. tso'apia' (grda-inlaw)

Algonkin

1. zinis (spfa)
2. ze'gozis (spmo)
3. dindawa (copa-inlaw)
4. na'angish (dahu)
5. na'angani'kwe (sowi)
6. ita (masihu-wibr)
7. dangwe (wobrwi-husi)
8. inim (sib-inlawoppsex)
   (avuncular?)
   (nepotic?)

Choctaw

1. haloka (sppa-chsp)
2. ipochi (wifa)
3. (hufa)
4. ipochi ohoyo (wimo)
5. (humo?)
6. imalak usi (wibr)
7. imalak usi ohoyo (wisi)
8. imombalaha (hubr)
9. ipo (husi)
10. imalak (sihu)
11. inhaiva (brwi)
12. iyup (dahu)
13. (sowi)
    (avuncular?)
    (nepotic?)

Kwakiutl

1. nagump (sppa-chsp;uncle, nephew)
2. q'ules (masihu?-mawibr?)
3. p'alwump (wobrwi-wohusi)
4. ginp (mabrsi-wisi)
5. (wosihu?-hubr)
6. selan (grpa-grch)
   (affinal uncle-
       stfa)
   (affinal aunt-
       stmo)

Zuni

1. talakyi (male inlaw)
2. ulani (female inlaw)

65

Yokuts

1. naxamis (spfa)
2. 'ontip (mo-spmo)
3. maksi (copa-inlaw)
4.   (dahu)
5. 'onmil (sowi)
6. 'idwap' (husi-wobrwi)
7. nepey (wibr-masihu)
8.   (hubr-mabrwi?)
9.   (wisi-wosihu?)
10. gitwinits' (husi)
11. nochi (wisihu)
12. tanaich (hubrwi)
13.   (wibrwi?)
14.   (husihu?)
          (avuncular?)
          (nepotic?)

DECEDENT KINSHIP

Chipewyan

1.   (strel-nuclear)
2.   (widower)
3.   (orphan)

Eskimo

1.   (strel-nuclear)

Shoshone

1.   (stfa)
2. doka (stmo)
3.   (stso)
4.   (stda)
5.   (stbr)
6.   (stsi)
7.   (widower)
8.   (widow)
9.   (orphan)

Sioux

1.   (stfa)
2.   (mastmo)
3. shankun (wostmo)
4. tawangan (stch)
5.   (stbr)
6.   (stsi)
7.   (widower)
8.   (widow)
9.   (orphan)

Algonkin

       (strel?)
1.   (widower)

Choctaw

1. inki toba (stfa)

66

Algonkin

2.   (widow)
3. ji'gam (widow of gens "brother"
4.   (orphan)

Choctaw

2. ishki toba (stmo)
3. ushi toba (stch)
4. ushi nakni toba (stso)
5. ushi tek toba (stda)
6. itibapishi toba (stbr)
7. intek toba (stsi)
8. itaiena (second wi)
9. ohoyoalhtakla (widower)
10. inhatak illi (widow)
11. alla alhtakla (orphan)

Kwakiutl

1. aewatsoe (stfa)
2. abatsoe (stmo)
3. xungoe (stch)
4.   (stsib)
5. magiłeam waqwa (hasib-oppsex)
6.   (hasibsamesex)
7.   (widower)
8.   (widow)
9. xama (orphan)

Zuni

1.   (stfa)
2. iniha (stmo)
3.   (stso)
4.   (stda)
5.   (stbr)
6.   (stsi)
7.   (widower)
8.   (widow)
9.   (orphan)

Yokuts

1.   (stfa)
2. mokoy (stmo)
3.   (stso)
4.   (stda)
5.   (stbr)
6.   (stsi)
7. tumyun (widowed)
8. holig (orphan)

OTHER ASCRIBED

Shoshone

1. chatika (newlywed)
2. kohiad (pregnant)

Sioux

1. chekpa (twin)
2. hunkaka (ancestor)

67

Shoshone

3. badikayu (pa of da)
4. duakuyu (pa of so)

Algonkin

1. bagwatushe (illegitimate)
2. widge (married)
3. de'komagan ɤala (relative)
4. gildzas (ancestor)
5. daniko'nojisha (descendant)
6. ki bagwatushe (mo of illegit.)
7. ugwatushe (fa of illegit.)

Choctaw

1. inki iksho (twin)
2. haiyup (unmarried)
3. ikauayo (bachelor)
4. tekchi iksho auaya alhpesa
   (marriageable woman)
5. ushi infohka (pregnant)
6. inkanomi (relative)
7. aiisht atiaka (progenitor)
8. intikba (maternal ancestor)
9. inki aiokla (paternal ancestor)
10. unchululi (descendant)

Kwakiutl

1. aɤ'ak (pregnant)

Yokuts

1. 'adeyas (twin)
2. ta'ati (relative)
3. yokochnim (distant relative)
4. heutoho (prostitute)
5. lowaitna (ma sex part-
   ner)
6. yiwin (wo sex partner)

MAGICO-RELIGIOUS

Chipewyan

1. inkoze (shaman)
2.   (witch)

Eskimo

1. angakok (shaman)
2. supillgoyok (curer)
3. anerillgoyok (curer)
4.   (juggler)
5. igugaun (witch)

Shoshone

1. puhagunt (shaman)
2. (antelope shaman)
3. (deer shaman)
4. (bear shaman)
5. (talker shaman)
6. timpi puhagunt (rock shaman)
7. ubu puhagunt (arrow shaman)
8. una dimpi puhagunt (rain shaman)
9. mukam puhagunt (spider shaman)
10. toxo puhagunt (rattlesnake shaman)
11. pa puhagunt (water shaman)
12. wa'a riv puhagunt (horse shaman)
13. (obstetric shaman)
14. ibi puhagunt (witch)
15. (novice)

Sioux

1. winchashta wakan (shaman)
2. pejuda winchashta (herbalist)

Algonkin

1. wabeno (shaman)
2. windigo (witch)
3. nanandawiiwe wanini (curer)
4. pachishka'owe (bloodletter)
5. paskikweige (bloodletter)
6. mashkikike wanini (herbalist)
7. kakanawenimit (midwife)
8. (funeral priest?)

Choctaw

1. holhkunna (shaman)
2. (buzzard shaman)
3. (owl shaman)
4. fappo (magician)
5. chuka ishi kanchak (witch)
6. ishtoholo (priest)
7. umba ikbi (rainmaker)
8. luak ikbi (firemaker)
9. kustush (pole planter)
10. na Yako fichi (curer)
11. alikchi (doctor)
12. (midwife?)
13. halalli (funeral manager)

Kwakiutl

1. paxala (shaman)
   2. (thrower shaman)
   3. (dreamer shaman)
   4. (feeler shaman)
   5. (sucking shaman)
   6. (soul shaman)
   7. naualaxs (magician)
8. eqasa (witch)
9. heliga (healer)
10. (society chief)
   11. telam (tribe's bait)
12. q'eqala (shaman's novice)

Zuni

1. (witch)
2. mosona (curing society director)
   3. (doctor)
   4. (midwife)
   5. (masseur)
6. shiwanni (priest)
   7. akwamosi (medicine water maker)
8. (plume waver?)
9. (salt pilgrim?)

Yokuts

1. 'antuw (shaman)
   2. mets 'antuw (power shaman)
   3. teshich gomom (weather shaman)
   4. noho'o (bear shaman)
   5. tu'udum (snake shaman)
   6. (doctor?)
   7. (midwife?)
8. hi'auta (shaman killer)
9. matanai wanamuts (jimsonweed leader)
10. chowe'ich (corpse handler)
   11. onotim (funeral woman)
   12. tonochim (burier)

ORACULAR RELIGIOUS

Chipewyan

1. nonti (prophet)
2. (singer)

Eskimo

(shaman)

Shoshone

1. muguanti (prophet)
2. hubi'eroti (singer)

Sioux

(shaman)
(singer)

Algonkin

1. kusabindugeyu (seer)
2. djisaki (diviner)
        (singer?)

Choctaw

hopaii (war prophet)
        (singer?)

Kwakiutl

1. doxts'as (seer)
2. naqate (singer)

Zuni

        (priest)
1. pupunakwe (choir)

Yokuts

1. kosana (prophet)
2. ahenich (singer)
3. 'ilaknihne (songmaker)

FETISHISTIC RELIGIOUS

Sioux

(drumkeeper)

Kwakiutl

mamats'enox (drumkeeper)

Zuni

(fetish guardian)

ECONOMIC TECHNOLOGY

Chipewyan

1. naze (hunter)
2.   (stalker)
3.   (trapper)
4.   (drummer)

Eskimo

1.   (hunter)
2.   (whale killer)
3.   (seal hunter)
4.   (harpooner)
5. niuyakti (steersman)
6.   (drummer)

Shoshone

1.   (hunter)
2.   (cook)
3.   (water carrier)

Sioux

1.   (hunter)
2.   (scout)
3.   (orderly)

71

Shoshone

4.   (drummer)

Sioux

4.   (food bearer)
(drumkeeper)
(pejuda winchashta, herb-
alist)

Algonkin

1.   (hunter)
2.   (fisherman)
3.   ("boy"-orderly)
4.   (berry picker)
5.   (rice gatherer)
   (herbalist)
   (midwife)

Choctaw

1. owatta (hunter)
2. nanabi (fisherman)
3. hokchi (planter)
4. ampo ikbi (potter)
5. aɫepa boli (drummer)
   (alikchi, doctor)
   (midwife?)

Kwakiutl

1.   (hunter)
2.   (bear hunter)
3. alewinoxu (sea hunter)
4. k'exk'axes (diver)
5. k'wax ala (steersman)
6.   (fisherman)
7.   (adzer)
8. ɫeq'enoxu (canoe builder)
9.   (woodcarver)
10. q'eq'altalgise (copper cut-
    ter)
11.   (weaver?)
12. yayaqat'enega (net
    weaver)
13. kinqalaɫala (food bearer)
    (heliga, healer)
    (midwife)
    (mamanats'enox, drumkeeper)

Zuni

1.   (hunter)
2.   (farmer)
3.   (gardener)
4.   (harvester)
5.   (potter)
6.   (weaver)
7.   (basketmaker)
8.   (drummer)
9. tehaitoynona (flautist)
10.   (beadmaker)
    (doctor)
    (masseur)
    (midwife)

Yokuts

1.   (hunter?)
2.   (deer stalker)
3.   (bear hunter)

72

4.   (basketmaker)
5.   (rattle shaker)
6.   (drummer?)
      (doctor)
      (midwife)

ECONOMIC OWNERSHIP

Eskimo

1. umialik (boat owner)
2. ilialuk (destitute)

Choctaw

(nobility)
1. tonksali (laborer)
2. ilbasha (poor man)
   (yuka, slave)
3. baska (gambler)
4. na kanchi (trader)

Kwakiutl

(chief)
1. wayapotala (noble)
2. gogwad (house owner)
3. nomadzil (retired)
4.   (worker)
      (slave)
5.   (trader?)

Zuni

1.   (rich)
2.   (laborer)
3.   (poor)
4.   (trader?)
5.   (auctioneer)
      (slave)

Yokuts

1. t'sow'ihni' (worker)
2.   (trader)

POLITICO-MILITARY

Chipewyan

1.   (warrior?)

Eskimo

1.   (warrior)

Shoshone

1. wiagait (brave)

Sioux

1.   (warrior?)

73

Shoshone	Sioux

2.   (scout)   2.   (scout?)
3. dirakone (police clown)   3. akichita (officer)

Algonkin	Choctaw

1. shimaganish (warrior)   1. nakni-tashka (warrior)
2. neodobine (scout)   2. atoni (guard)
3. okichita (brave)

Kwakiutl	Zuni

1. winax (warrior)   (koyemshi, clown)
2. ts'ats'ekila (watchman)   1. pit/ashiwanni (warrior)

Yokuts

1.   (warrior?)

POLITICAL AUTHORITY

Chipewyan	Eskimo

Civil: Civil:
 1.   (headman)   1. pimain (headman)
         (people)   2. kivrarniaktuna (herald)
Religious: (people)
      (inkoze, shaman) Religious:
 2.   (dancer)   (angakok, shaman)
Military: 3. (dancer)
 3.   (war leader)   4. qailertetang (masked
      (warrior?)   dancer)
Economic: 5. mirqussang (masked
 4.   (hunt leader)   dancer)
      (naze, hunter)   (people)
                    Military:
                  6. issumautang (leader)
                    (warrior)
                  Economic:
                    (niuyakti, steersman)
                    (hunter)
                  Recreational?:

74

7. (narrator)
   (people)

Shoshone

Civil:
 1. pakw'navi (chief)
 2. pataivo (headman)
 3. tegwani (speaker)
    (people)
Religious:
 4. kwini tegwani (dance
       speaker)
 5. (dancer)
    (people)
Military:
 6. navedink tegwani (war
       speaker)
    (warrior)
Economic:
 7. tugu tegwani (hunt speaker)
 8. (pine nut speaker)
 9. (rabbit hunt speaker)
    (hunter)
Liaison:
    (chief)
10. (messenger)
    (speaker)
Dispute:
    (headman)
11. (go-between)
    (headman)

Sioux

Civil:
 1. wishasa itashan (chief)
 2. wakishun (headman)
 3. wakishunza (elder)
 4. (crier)
    (people)
Religious:
 5. gaje (dance leader)
 6. opaje (society member)
    (orderly)
    (people)
Military:
 7. shannunpa tawa (war lead-
       er)
 8. akichita itashan (officer)
    (warrior)
 9. (orderly)
Economic:
10. winchabasi (hunt leader)
11. wanyacho (hunt judge)
12. waiyuta (hunt rationer)
    (hunter)
Coordinative:
    (chief or dance leader)
13. shankpamini (herald)
    (people)

Algonkin

Civil:
 1. (chief)
 2. ogima (headman)
 3. (elder)
 4. (crier)
    (people)

Choctaw

Civil:
 1. minko (chief)
 2. minko imohoyo (chief's
       wife)
 3. peʎichi (headman)
 4. anampuli (elder)

Algonkin

Religious:
5. nigani (ritual leader)
6. mijenoe (assistant)
   (shimaganish, warrior)
   (oshkabewis, orderly)
         (assistant)
         (assistant)
         (assistant)
         (assistant)
7. windigokan (cannibal dancer)
   (people)
Military:
8. meyosi (war leader)
   (okichita, brave)
   (shimaganish, warrior)
   (oshkabewis, boy)
Economic:
   (?)
   (hunter)
Coordinative:
   (chief or priest)
9. ("steersman")
   (people)

Choctaw

5. fani minko (calumet chief)
   (people)
Religious:
6. archimagi (high priest)
   (ishtoholo, priest)
7. hiƚa (dancer)
   (people)
Military:
   (hopaii, war prophet)
8. alhtoka (officer)
   (nakni-tashka, warrior)
9. imataha (novice)
Economic:
   (?)
   (farmer or hunter)
Coordinative:
   (chief or priest)
10. tishu minko (speaker)
    (people)
Liaison:
    (chief)
11. anumpa shali (messenger)
    (priest)
Dispute:
    (anampuli, elder)
12. nan aiyachi (go-between)
    (anampuli, elder)

Kwakiutl

Civil:
1. (head chief)
2. gigame (chief)
3. oema (chief's wife)
4. ƚawulqamaya (chief's son)
5. k'edeƚ (chief's daughter)
6. giqamene (chief's family)
7. xamagame (headman)

Zuni

Civil (Theocratic):
1. kiakwemosi mosona (north rain priest)
2. (assistant north rain priest)
3. onnawa mosona (south rain priest)
4. paƚto mosona (east rain priest)

Kwakiutl	Zuni

<table>
<tr><td>

Kwakiutl

8. giaga̲ɬ (elder)
9. q'ap'aenoxu (assembler)
   (people)
Religious:
10. (society chief)
11. guanuɬame (attendant)
12. senat (dancer)
   13. (dancer's attendant)
      (people)
Shamanism:
14. paxame (head shaman)
   (paxala, shaman)
   (q'eqala, novice)
Military:
   (?)
   (winax, warrior)
Economic:
   (k'waxɬala, steersman)
   (fisherman)
Coordinative:
   (chief or society chief)
15. alkwasa gigamayexa
   (speaker)
   (people)
Liaison:
   (chief)
16. hoɬaq'is (messenger)
   17. xixiqala (seal inviter)
   18. kaqaule (cannibal invit-
      er)
   19. aɬo'lsala (seal inviter
      speaker)
   20. nawulqalagilis (cannibal
      inviter speaker)
   (society chief)

</td><td>

Zuni

5. koyemshi mosona (west
   rain priest)
6. sontalu (older brother bow
   priest)
7. (younger brother bow
   priest)
8. we'ashonna (crier)
   (people)
Religious:
   (shiwanni, priest)
9. (associate priest)
10. (assistant priest)
11. alunakwe (manager)
12. otaikya (dancer)
   (people)
Religious Society:
13. mosona (director)
   (tikyili, member)
Kiva:
14. worli (manager)
   (kiva member)
Military:
   (bow priest)
   (pitɬashiwanni, warrior)
Economic:
15. (ditch boss)
   (farmer?)
Coordinative:
   (chief, priest, society di-
      rector)
16. pekwin (speaker)
   (pitɬashiwanni, warrior)
   (koyemshi, clown-police)
   (people)
Liaison:
   (chief)
17. alunakwe (messengers)
   (priest)

</td></tr>
</table>

Civil:
1. tiya (chief)
2. tuye'i (headman)
3. pineti (elder)
4. winatum (crier)
   (people)
Religious:
   (hi'auta, shaman killer)
   ('antuw, shaman)
5. wodyo (dancer)
   6. huhuna (owl dancer)
   (people)
Military:
   (?)
   (warrior?)
Economic:
   (?)
   (hunter?)
Coordinative:
   (chief or shaman)
7. di'ele (speaker)
   (people)
Liaison:
   (chief)
8. hoyelis (messenger)
   (shaman)

POLITICAL OWNERSHIP

Chipewyan	Shoshone
(warrior)	(wiagiat, brave)
1. (slave)	1. (slave)

Sioux	Algonkin
(warrior?)	(shimaganish, warrior)
1. (slave?)	1. (slave?)

Choctaw	Kwakiutl

Choctaw

(nakni-tashka, warrior)
1. yuka (slave)

Kwakiutl

1. gigi (master)
2. q'ako (slave)
   (gigame, chief)
3. gigad (chief's people)

Zuni

(pitɬashiwanni, warrior)
1.   (slave?)

Yokuts

(warrior?)
1.   (slave?)

Bibliography

Boas, Franz. 1888. The Central Eskimo. Sixth Annual Report of the Bureau of American Ethnology: 399-669.
-------. 1897. The Social Organization and Secret Societies of the Kwakiutl Indians. Report of the United States National Museum for 1895: 311-738.
-------. 1921. The Ethnology of the Kwakiutl, based on data collected by George Hunt. Thirty-fifth Annual Report of the Bureau of American Ethnology: 43-794.
-------. 1925. Contributions to the Ethnology of the Kwakiutl. Columbia University Contributions to Anthropology 3.
-------. 1930. The Religion of the Kwakiutl Indians. Columbia University Contributions to Anthropology 10 (1, 2).
Brown, Paula. 1952. Changes in Ojibwa Social Control. American Anthropologist 54:57-70.
Bunzel, Ruth L. 1932a. Introduction to Zuñi Ceremonialism. Forty-seventh Annual Report of the Bureau of American Ethnology: 467-544.
-------. 1932b. Zuñi Katcinas. Forty-seventh Annual Report of the Bureau of American Ethnology: 837-1086.
Bushnell, David I., Jr. 1909. The Choctaw of Bayou Lacomb, St. Tammany Parish, Louisiana. Bureau of American Ethnology Bulletin Number 48.
Byington, Cyrus. 1915. A Dictionary of the Choctaw Language. Bureau of American Ethnology Bulletin Number 46.
Durkheim, Emile. 1947. Division of Labor in Society. The Free Press, Glencoe, Illinois.
Eggan, Frederick R. 1937. Historical Changes in the Choctaw Kinship System. American Anthropologist 39:34-52.

--------. 1950. Social Organization of the Western Pueblos. University of Chicago Press, Chicago.

Gayton, Anne H. 1930. Yokuts-Mono Chiefs and Shamans. University of California Publications in American Archaeology and Ethnology 24 (8).

--------. 1948. Yokuts and Western Mono Ethnography. University of California Anthropological Records 10 (1).

Gladwin, Thomas. 1948. Comanche Kin Behavior. American Anthropologist 50:73-94.

Hassrick, Royal B. 1944. Teton Dakota Kinship System. American Anthropologist 46:338-47.

Hoebel, E. Adamson. 1939. Comanche and H3kandika Shoshone Relationship Systems. American Anthropologist 41: 440-57.

--------. 1940. The Political Organization and Law-Ways of the Comanche Indians. American Anthropological Association Memoirs 54.

Honigmann, John J. 1946. Ethnography and Acculturation of the Fort Nelson Slave. Yale University Publications in Anthropology 33.

--------. 1949. Culture and Ethos of Kaska Society. Yale University Publications in Anthropology 40.

Jenness, Diamond. 1935. The Ojibwa Indians of Parry Island, Their Social and Religious Life. Canada Department of Mines Bulletin 78, Anthropological Series 17.

Kroeber, Alfred L. 1917. Zuñi Kin and Clan. Anthropological Papers of the American Museum of Natural History 18.

--------. 1925. Handbook of the Indians of California. Bureau of American Ethnology Bulletin 78.

--------. 1939. Cultural and Natural Areas of Native North America. University of California Publications in American Archaeology and Ethnology 38.

Landes, Ruth. 1937. Ojibwa Sociology. Columbia University Contributions to Anthropology 29.

Lévi-Strauss, Claude. 1949. Les structures élémentaires de la parenté. Presses Universitaires de France, Paris.

--------. 1951. Language and the Analysis of Social Laws. American Anthropologist 53:155-63.

Linton, Ralph. 1936. The Study of Man. Appleton, New York and London.

Lowie, Robert H. 1909. The Assiniboine. Anthropological Papers of the American Museum of Natural History 4 (1).

--------. 1913. Dance Associations of the Eastern Dakota. Anthropological Papers of the American Museum of Natural History 11 (2).

--------. 1915. Dances and Societies of the Plains Shoshone. Anthropological Papers of the American Museum of Natural History 11 (10).

--------. 1920. Primitive Society. Liveright, New York.

--------. 1948. Social Organization. Rinehart, New York.

Maine, Henry J. S. 1873. Ancient Law. Holt, New York.

Mason, J. Alden. 1946. Notes on the Indians of the Great Slave Lake Area. Yale University Publications in Anthropology 34.

Morgan, Lewis H. 1870. Systems of Consanguinity and Affinity of the Human Family. Smithsonian Contributions to Knowledge 17:1-590. Washington, D.C.

Moses, Lincoln E. 1952. Non-Parametric Statistics for Psychological Research. Psychological Bulletin 49:122-43.

Murdock, George P. 1949. Social Structure. Macmillan, New York.

Newman, Stanley. 1944. The Yokuts Language of California. Viking Fund Publications in Anthropology 2.

Parsons, Elsie Clews. 1933. Hopi and Zuñi Ceremonialism. American Anthropological Association Memoirs 39.

Parsons, Talcott. 1951. The Social System. The Free Press, Glencoe, Illinois.

Radin, Max. 1934. Status. Encyclopedia of the Social Sciences 14:373-77. Macmillan, New York.

Rasmussen, Knud. 1931. The Netsilik Eskimos: Social Life and Spiritual Culture. Report of the Fifth Thule Expedition, 1921-1924: 8 (1-2).

Skinner, Alanson. 1911. Notes on the Eastern Cree and Northern Salteaux. Anthropological Papers of the American Museum of Natural History 9 (1).

--------. 1914. Political Organizations, Cults and Ceremonies of the Plains-Ojibway and Plains-Cree Indians. Anthropological Papers of the American Museum of Natural History 11 (6).

Speck, Frank G. 1915. Family Hunting Territories and Social Life of Various Algonkin Bands of the Ottawa Valley. Canada Geological Survey Memoirs 70, Anthropological Series 8.

Spier, Leslie. 1925. The Distribution of Kinship Systems in

North America. University of Washington Publications in Anthropology 1:69-88.

Stefansson, Vilhjalmur. 1919. The Stefansson-Anderson Arctic Expedition of the American Museum: Preliminary Ethnological Report. Anthropological Papers of the American Museum of Natural History 14 (1).

Stevenson, Matilda Coxe. 1904. The Zuñi Indians: Their Mythology, Esoteric Fraternities and Ceremonies. Twenty-third Annual Report of the Bureau of American Ethnology: 3-608.

Steward, Julian H. 1938. Basin-Plateau Aboriginal Sociopolitical Groups. Bureau of American Ethnology Bulletin 120.

Swanton, John R. 1911. Indian Tribes of the Lower Mississippi Valley and Adjacent Coast of the Gulf of Mexico. Bureau of American Ethnology Bulletin 43.

-------. 1918. An Early Account of the Choctaw Indians. American Anthropological Association Memoirs 5 (2).

-------. 1931. Source Material for the Social and Ceremonial Life of the Choctaw Indians. Bureau of American Ethnology Bulletin 103.

-------. 1945. The Indian Tribes of North America. Bureau of American Ethnology Bulletin 145.

Walker, J. R. 1917. The Sun Dance and Other Ceremonies of the Oglala Division of the Teton Dakota. Anthropological Papers of the American Museum of Natural History 16 (2).

Warner, W. Lloyd and Paul S. Lunt. 1942. The Status System of a Modern Community. Yale University Press, New Haven.

Wissler, Clark. 1912. Societies and Ceremonial Associations in the Oglala Division of the Teton Dakota. Anthropological Papers of the American Museum of Natural History 11 (1).

Law and Status among the Kiowa Indians. Jane Richardson. (Monograph I) 1940. 142 pages, bibliography. Out of print

Rank and Warfare among the Plains Indians. Bernard Mishkin. (Monograph III) 1940. 73 pages, bibliography. Out of print

Disease, Religion and Society in the Fiji Islands. Dorothy M. Spencer. (Monograph II) 1941. 92 pages, chart. Out of print

An Analysis of Inca Militarism. Joseph Bram. (Monograph IV) 1941. 93 pages, bibliography. $1.50

A Primitive Mexican Economy. George M. Foster. (Monograph V) 1942. 123 pages, plates, maps, bibliography. Out of print

The Effects of White Contact upon Blackfoot Culture, with Special Reference to the Role of the Fur Trade. Oscar Lewis. (Monograph VI) 1942. 79 pages, maps, bibliography. $1.50

Arapesh. R. F. Fortune. (Publication XIX) 1942. 243 pages. $5.00

Prayer: The Compulsive Word. Gladys A. Reichard. (Monograph VII) 1944. 121 pages, figures, bibliography. $2.50

Changing Configurations in the Social Organization of a Blackfoot Tribe during the Reserve Period (The Blood of Alberta, Canada). Esther S. Goldfrank. (Monograph VIII, bound with IX) 1945. 81 pages, plates, bibliography. $2.50

Observations on Northern Blackfoot Kinship. L. M. Hanks, Jr., and Jane Richardson. (Monograph IX, bound with VIII) 1945. 37 pages, figures. $2.50

Map of North American Indian Languages. Compiled and drawn by C. F. Voegelin and E. W. Voegelin. (Publication XX) 1945. Wall size, color. $2.00

The Influence of Islam on a Sudanese Religion. Joseph Greenberg. (Monograph X) 1946. 83 pages, figures, map, bibliography. $2.50

Alaskan Eskimo Ceremonialism. Margaret Lantis. (Monograph XI) 1947. 143 pages, maps, bibliography. $2.75

Economics of the Mount Hagen Tribes, New Guinea. Abraham L. Gitlow. (Monograph XII) 1947. 122 pages, plates, figures, maps, bibliography. $2.75

Ceremonial Patterns in the Greater Southwest. Ruth M. Underhill. (Monograph XIII, bound with XIV) 1948. 74 pages, bibliography, index. $2.50

Factionalism in Isleta Pueblo. David H. French. (Monograph XIV, bound with XIII) 1948. 54 pages, bibliography. $2.50

The Negro in Northern Brazil: A Study in Acculturation. Octavio da Costa Eduardo. (Monograph XV) 1948. 139 pages, map, bibliography. $2.75

Bali: Rangda and Barong. Jane Belo. (Monograph XVI) 1949. 71 pages, plates, figures, bibliography. $2.75

The Rubber-Ball Games of the Americas. Theodore Stern. (Monograph XVII) 1950. 129 pages, plate, maps, bibliography. $2.50

Fighting with Property: A Study of Kwakiutl Potlatching and Warfare 1792-1930. Helen Codere. With Tribal and Linguistic Map of Vancouver Island and Adjacent Territory, drawn and compiled by Vincent F. Kotschar. (Monograph XVIII) 1950. 143 pages, figures, maps, charts, bibliography. $3.00

The Cheyenne in Plains Indian Trade Relations 1795-1840. Joseph Jablow. (Monograph XIX) 1951. 110 pages, maps, bibliography, index. $2.50

The Tsimshian: Their Arts and Music. The Tsimshian and Their Neighbors, by Viola E. Garfield; Tsimshian Sculpture, by Paul S. Wingert; Tsimshian Songs, by Marius Barbeau. (Publication XVIII) 1951. 302 pages, plates, figures, maps, music, bibliography, index. $6.00

Navaho Grammar. Gladys A. Reichard. (Publication XXI) 1951. 407 pages, bibliography. $7.00

Buzios Island: A Caiçara Community in Southern Brazil. Emilio Willems in cooperation with Gioconda Mussolini. (Monograph XX) 1952. 124 pages, figures, maps, bibliography. $2.75

Chichicastenango: A Guatemalan Village. Ruth Bunzel. (Publication XXII) 1952. 464 pages, figures, bibliography. $7.00

Changing Military Patterns on the Great Plains (17th Century through Early 19th Century). Frank Raymond Secoy. (Monograph XXI) 1953. 120 pages, maps, bibliography. $2.75

Bali: Temple Festival. Jane Belo. (Monograph XXII) 1953. 78 pages, plates, chart, bibliography. $2.75

Hungarian and Vogul Mythology. Géza Róheim. With appendixes by John Lotz. (Monograph XXIII) 1954. 96 pages, map, bibliography. $2.75

The Trumaí Indians of Central Brazil. Robert F. Murphy and Buell Quain. (Monograph XXIV) 1955. 120 pages, plates, map, bibliography. $2.75

The Deeply Rooted: A Study of a Drents Community in the Netherlands. John Y. Keur and Dorothy L. Keur. (Monograph XXV) 1955. 208 pages, plates, maps, bibliography. $3.00

The Tlingit Indians: Results of a Trip to the Northwest Coast of America and the Bering Straits. Aurel Krause. Translated by Erna Gunther. 1956. 320 pages, plates, figures, map, bibliography, index. $4.50

Village and Plantation Life in Northeastern Brazil. Harry William Hutchinson. 1957. 209 pages, plates, maps, charts, bibliography, index. $4.50

Malaya. Norton Ginsburg and Chester F. Roberts, Jr. 1958. 547 pages, maps, charts, bibliography, index. $6.00

Social Stratification in Polynesia. Marshall D. Sahlins. 1958. 306 pages, figures, bibliography. $4.50

Status Terminology and the Social Structure of North American Indians. Munro S. Edmonson. 1958. 92 pages, charts, bibliography. $3.00